DISCARD

DANGEROUS
DE–LIAISONS

JEAN-MÁRIE COLOMBANI
& WALTER WELLS

DANGEROUS
DE–LIAISONS

What's Really Behind
the War Between
France and the U.S.

Edited by Luc Jacob-Duvernet

MELVILLE HOUSE PUBLISHING
HOBOKEN, NEW JERSEY

©2004 MELVILLE HOUSE PUBLISHING
ORIGINALLY PUBLISHED IN FRENCH AS *DÉLIAISONS DANGEREUSES*
©2004 ÉDITIONS JACOB-DUVERNET

TRANSLATION OF JEAN-MARIE COLOMBANI'S TEXT FOR THE ENGLISH VERSION
BY SARAH ALEXANDER.

SINCERE THANKS TO THOSE WHO PARTICIPATED IN THE MAKING OF THIS BOOK:
FRANÇOISE TRICARD AND SANDRINE DE LACLOS, DENIS GEFFROY AND
BÉATRICE DE GASQUET.

MELVILLE HOUSE PUBLISHING
P.O. BOX 3278
HOBOKEN, NJ   07030

BOOK DESIGN: DAVID KONOPKA

FIRST EDITION / MARCH 2004
ISBN: 0-9746078-5-1

LIBRARY OF CONGRESS CIP DATA ON FILE.

Contents

Foreword

For a year now, there has been a crisis in French-American relations. The virulence in the discourse of political leaders—related by the media with a total lack of nuance—is as worrisome as it is disturbing. All too often, insults have overridden dialogue; distrust now seems to be the only thread binding the two nations.

Is the American war in Iraq sufficient cause to explain the magnitude of the current crisis? Suddenly rekindled after September 11, 2001, did the wealth of sympathy benefiting the United States in France merely evaporate around Iraqi oil wells, or is this just another episode in a long-term game of cat and mouse? A long run of passion, remission, sudden or compounded hate? One might be led to believe that in fact, between an economic, military superpower like the United States and a cultural superpower like France, the similarities conflict with the disparities to a degree making the two cultures irreconcilable.

If "differences" seem to dominate French-American relations today, we must not lose sight of an alliance over two centuries old, the strong ties that bind France and the US, and the mutual fascination of the two nations. Nor should we fall into the trap of an angelic blissfulness that blinds us to the conflicts and basic differences that divide the two countries. Somewhere between such naiveté and cynicism, there must be room for a more subtle, if not more honest, analysis.

To write about America and French-American relations is a perilous endeavor. Former French Ambassador to the United States Jacques Andreani wrote in the introduction of his work *L'Amerique et nous* (*America and Us*), "No speech about America is neutral. Whether explicit or implicit, those who talk about it take sides. Their judgment is often formulated in terms of total success or total failure." What's more: "French speech is the least neutral of all."[1] To claim objectivity in the flood of passionate reactions that have characterized the last months would constitute an illusion. But may one be satisfied with Manichaean visions which are all too often one-sided? Certainly not!

Following discussions with Jean-Marie Colombani, Director of the French daily *Le Monde*, and Walter Wells, Executive Editor of *The International Herald Tribune*, it seemed to us that dialogue would be most likely to produce an accurate analysis. Over the course of our discussions, it became apparent that the French-American crisis is deeper than anyone would like to think. And neither the strategic changes in the Bush administration since September 2003, nor the difficulties encountered by the American Army in Iraq, have modified the givens. The accumulated resentment remains. Hence it appeared necessary to us, if not even indispensable, to begin exploring the French-American disagreement, in the form of a cordial debate between Jean-Marie Colombani and Walter Wells. Many questions were raised over the course of the meetings, which took place for the most part in Paris during the summer of 2003, with the participation of the young historian, Denis Geffroy, who provided research, and helped prepare the questions and organize the discussions, all of which was key to structuring the overall dialogue.

The authors have chosen their most pertinent analyses for this book. How can one explain the virulence of anti-American and Francophobic sentiment? What has been the responsibility of the two presidents and their entourage during the current crisis? Beyond the disagreement over the war in Iraq, what are the values and interests that unite or divide France and the United States? Is the "benevolent hegemony" of the American empire inevitable on the horizon of the contemporary world? Should Europe be an ally, partner or counter-balance of the US? Does the current argument hide reciprocal admiration and fascination on the part of the two nations? Finally, what are the conditions necessary for restoring a peaceful relationship, a serene and sincere partnership, a loyal and reinforced cooperation, between France and America?

Any friendship based on ignorance, indifference, or condescension can only incite crisis, misunderstanding, and resentment. More than ever, we must renew dialogue. Therein lies the purpose of this book of conversations: the hope to promote friendship between two nations that remain—in spite of whatever anyone may believe or say—profoundly united.

Luc Jacob-Duvernet

Dangerous De-Liaisons

1
Sources of Anti-Americanism and Francophobia

"September 11, 2001. French citizens gather by the thousands in front of the American Embassy. They assemble spontaneously to express solidarity with a nation struck by terrorism. The next day, the daily newspaper *Le Monde* described this spirit in an editorial entitled 'We are all Americans.' Jacques Chirac promised to lend support to the United States and on September 18 became the first head of state to visit George W. Bush after the attacks. The international press covered the visit extensively. At the dawn of this new period in their common history, French-American relations hit their peak. The spirits of Lafayette, Pershing and the liberators of Normandy seem to dominate the two countries once again. But the honeymoon was brief," said Justin Vaisse, just one year ago.[2]

February 2003: waves of anti-Americanism and Francophobia overtake France and the United States. The debate on appropriateness and possible forms of military intervention in Iraq puts the two governments in violent opposition. Wild accusations, pat responses and mud-slinging animate press and media to the detriment of accurate, honest, justified criticism. To support their points of view, both sides revert to standard, worn-out prejudices and clichés of anti-Americanism and Francophobia. In the eyes of the Bush administration and the American press corps, France is perceived as an unfaithful ally, recalcitrant, arrogant, unpredictable, and the French appear unfailingly ungrateful, anti-Semitic, and weak, like "cheese-eating surrender monkeys."[3] The inhabitants of the "old Europe"[4] are referred to as Euro-pygmies. On the other hand, French intellectuals view President Bush as the ultimate caricature of the Yankee Philistine, a fundamental Puritan, falling into the same traps.

Personal enmities, diverging viewpoints of the French and American governments on policy in Iraq, as well as governance of the planet, do not suffice, however, to explain this eruption of passion and resentment. French anti-Americanism, and American Francophobia, have become part of each country's makeup.

WALTER WELLS: From the starting point of September 11, 2001, it's not just the difference over Iraq and over 1441[5] that got us to the crisis. The personalities of both presidents, Bush and Chirac, played significant roles. An element no doubt is that both men have a predisposition not to like the other. Chirac: worldly, senior to Bush and with a lifetime of experience as a politician, much of it successful. And let's not leave out condescending. His lecture to the "new Europeans" confirmed that as part of his nature.

And on the other side, there is Bush, relatively young, relatively inexperienced, not sophisticated, and, in Chirac's view, in need of a mentor. It was a God-given chance for France to play the role it has always wanted to play—to coach the American president. But in this instance we weren't worshiping the same God.

There's another thing about Bush and I think it's crucial here. A distrust of the French is almost in the American DNA, and certainly in the DNA of someone who is less worldly and less traveled, who has never been engaged by the French on any kind of personal level, whether it's visiting the Louvre, dining in a three-star restaurant or coming to France for the classic junior year abroad. And there's basically no French element in the American melting pot, no votes to solicit, no Bastille Day parade down Fifth Avenue for him to lead.

There is a perceived French aloofness from America's haphazard domestic life, and that has contributed to a distrust by my countrymen toward your country. Now we could talk for years about whether that distrust is merited, and about the events that have contributed to it, but let's not hide from the fact that it's very basic to the American psyche. Even in 1945 the US military authorities in France issued a guide for the GI's in the occupying force responding to the kinds of routine criticisms that you could hear today on Fox or read in the *New York Post*.

But aside from the very different personalities, there was also the fact that America made its purpose and intentions clear from the outset, and France thought that America's course could be manipulated. Given the straightforwardness on the American side, and the efforts at manipulation by the French, and given the nature of the two presidents, the split was unavoidable.

The American position may have been simplistic and it could even have been wrong—a lot of Americans thought it was wrong and thought even that Bush himself was evil. But right or wrong, it was unambiguous. The French expected Powell to carry more weight within the administration, and their attempt to use him to alter American policy, to modify the intention, was a very, very major misreading of the situation, and it resulted in the perception in the administration that France was not straightforward and, even worse, that the French were duplicitous.

JEAN-MARIE COLOMBANI: Was the French position really not clear? What role does man play in this? I am not totally convinced that the divorce was "inevitable." In the beginning, they were made for each other. The French right has always used the

American right as a role model. The fact that it wins in the United States, always reinforces the conservative camp here. In addition, the fact that Bush has adopted an orthodox Gaullist position with regards to the United Nations should have brought the two nations closer together. Don't forget de Gaulle denounced the " machine" and discounted administrative supervision à la "United Nations" over the affairs of the world. After September 11, Chirac was the first to fly over the ruins of the disaster, and it was immediately thought that the French president had opted for privileged relations with Bush. Moreover Chirac continually evoked his own style: "As a young student I spent a year in the United States, I came to know American life, I worked there. I am just like you, one of yours." Interviewed by Larry King, he created a persona speaking perfect English, at home with American culture, in a style similar to American polticians today, direct and warm. Whether on an ideological, personal or circumstantial level, these three elements provided the basis for good understanding between Chirac and Bush.

How did it all go awry? The way in which the French position was expressed was probably not clear. There were two distinct phases. The first which I just described, beginning September 12, 2001; the second when the American intention to attack Iraq became apparent. Chirac came to believe that Bush is a dangerous man; dangerous because he represents the minority point of view in the United States and because he expresses it in a rather sectarian manner. Chirac was probably playing both sides: one position in front of his interlocuter and behind the scenes, his reflections becoming more and more critical, even more concerned. I admit that on Chirac's part, there may have been ambiguity in allowing the United States to believe that ultimately France would participate, while pursuing a completely different path leading to the split at which we arrive today.

WELLS: Bush is not without critics in the United States, severe critics. Bill Keller, who supported the war, wrote in a column (before he was named editor of the *New York Times*): "Even if you believe this war is justified, the route to it has been an ugly display of American opportunism and bullying, dissembling and dissonance."[6]

Those are harsh accusations and you could make them in spades now, especially given the questions about American and British intelligence before the war. Credibility is Bush's Achilles heel, and that explains why he has been pushed into a defensive crouch, no doubt because it's clear-cut and easy for voters to understand. "He lied," his opponents will be able to say. Or perhaps they will be a little more accurate and nuanced: "He allowed lies to be used in his argument for going to war." They have already started saying it, in fact.

The dissonance is growing and, in fact, what the British press called the "dodgy dossier" is a point of weakness for Bush, not just Tony Blair. And Bush faces election first.

But that wasn't the case before the bombing began. There was no vulnerability at all then. And it's a very big mistake to think that Bush's determination to go to war had only minority support. Americans back their president in a crisis, and they back him in foreign policy because he is supposed to know more than they do. And they always, always support intervention abroad—until they stop supporting it, as in Vietnam. And frankly it was easy enough to convince the public—still traumatized by 9/11—that removing Saddam Hussein was the next essential battle in the war against terrorism, and essential too in paving the way to peace in the Middle East.

Also, there is the historical issue of American exceptionalism. We are a people who see ourselves as always doing good when we fight abroad. We are the liberators, we protect the weak and preserve the innocent. You think that's naïve, or worse. But again, you're practically talking about the DNA code. Criticising that is almost equivalent to criticising the French because the average height is 5'7", or whatever it is, and not 6'.

So Chirac and Villepin may have thought that Iraq was folly, but if they thought it was folly in the eyes of the American electorate, that it fell outside that sense of obligation and exceptionalism, or that it was merely a problem-ridden initiative by a minority president, their perceptions couldn't have been further off base.

And when the French allowed themselves to be cast in the position of protecting Saddam Hussein against the historical American mission to do good, to protect and to liberate, then the schoolyard meanness that we all have in us started the name-calling.

I'd like to come back to the point I raised earlier about the predisposition of both men to dislike each other. Do you remember the incident at the G7 summit in Denver when Clinton was president? As is the custom, the president of the host country, Clinton, gave a gift to each of the other national leaders. The tradition is to make a gift of symbolic significance. And Clinton's gift was a pair of cowboy boots. As I recall, Chirac was openly dismissive of the gift as gauche, as unsophisticated.

That suggested to me at the time that despite all of his pretense of being nearly Americanized himself, of having sold ice-cream and eaten hamburgers and spent vacations in the American heartland, perhaps there was more than a note of dismissiveness and arrogance by Chirac toward American iconography. There certainly wasn't a recognition of those icons, nor was there respect for the maxim that it's not the gift but the thought that counts.

On the opposite side, I am certain—without knowing Bush obviously—I am certain that he is dismissive of Chirac and perhaps of the entire French nation as effete, snobbish, and self-important. I say that with certitude because those gentler aspects of masculine behaviour, if ever nascent in an American boy, get pounded out of him on the playground by the age of 6. Certainly those aspects are very foreign to Bush—a man who apparently thinks Crawford, Texas, is the center of the universe, who must not have had much curiosity about the world because he never set out to see very much of it.

There's no doubt of Bush's political instincts or sophistication as a survivor—he's a fighter and he's mostly a winner. But he's certainly not worldly. And who knows, maybe because of that there's some social insecurity. Not to indulge in long-distance psychoanalysis, as tempting as it often is to do so: One way of expressing insecurity is to be dismissive of people who threaten in any way. Now did Chirac's sophistication, his "Frenchness," somehow threaten our macho man from Crawford? Clearly his condescension offended Bush and his entourage.

I do not know of any points of personal disrespect between the two men, but I do think that when it came to Iraq, the fact that France was resistant—that even before we got to a vote in the UN on war against Iraq France tried very hard to prevent NATO assistance to Turkey, facing a potential Iraqi threat, that France resisted in the UN and campaigned for its own client states, in Africa, to resist also—set off a very big chain reaction. America— big, rich, powerful, accustomed to having its own way—how is it going to react? Might it just be with anger and dismissiveness and even name-calling?

COLOMBANI: Oddly enough, both men probably have the same concept of politics: Both are clan men, who know the brutality of public life. Arrogance is probably another of their common points. Chirac's arrogance is obvious: When the French president used to speak with his European counterparts about the new American government—before September 11—he couldn't find words harsh enough. The ensuing discourse was in essence, succinct: "Listen," he would say to his visitors, "it's really very simple. Americans are stupid bastards; if you want to know what to do, just do the exact opposite of what they suggest." From that stemmed the French reality: Our president talks like yours! As for arrogance, Bush takes the prize. This is particulary true about Europe. The perfect Europe, according to Bush, is the relationship he maintains with Silvio Berlusconi: a clan leader with his puppet. And from that point of view, whether it be Chirac or anyone else, no French president can adhere to that vision. No German, no Frenchman, no Englishman.

To come back to the boots incident, Chirac has constructed his public persona on the image of the nice guy, simple and absolutely not cultivated. The reality however, is just opposite: He is very cultivated, very complex and in politics, a killer. Hence he would have been flattered if Bush had offered him twelve volumes of an unknown Chinese poet to prove that true leaders know what he is all about. And if the truth be told, everything is political. He has become trapped in his own image. He is cultivated and slightly snobbish. When Chirac was Mayor of Paris, he hit rock bottom. No one believed in him any more, so I used to go visit him. He would have people over on Sunday and don astonishing apparel: a sweatsuit. The official sweatsuit of the French football or rugby team, projecting the image of a warm man, close to the people. But when you looked at his feet, he was wearing gold-embroidered slippers. The true Chirac is also what he has on his feet, and like most of the French bourgeoisie, he is attracted to bourgeois standards. But the image he projects first is the sweatsuit. He is always wearing a mask. And he didn't appreciate the fact that someone mirrored the public image of the simple man which he created for himself. The basic paradox is that Bush is victim of the same stereotypes as Chirac: Like Reagan before him, the French quickly treated him like some negligible quantity, like someone who according to Hubert Vedrine, former French Foreign Minister, could only produce "simplistic" thought. Wrong. With Bush, Chirac has fallen into his own trap.

WELLS: I'm pretty sure that Bush doesn't have any embroidered bedroom slippers. And if he ever received any as a gift, I suspect they'd be put away with Chirac's cowboy boots!

COLOMBANI: To sum up these men and their personalities, one must admit that Chirac has a short coming: he is not a strategist. He lacks vision, projects. But he does have one quality: reacting swiftly. Take Bosnia for example, where fortunately he took a stand contrary to François Mitterrand's policy of immobility, because he felt it was intolerable that French soldiers in the UN blue helmets be humiliated over there. He would have been a brilliant marshall in the Empire. Except that there's no longer an Emperor. But he is not ready to admit that the Emperor could be Texan! The presidents are not alone in provoking the degeneration of French-American relations. We also have to take a look at the role played by their entourage.

WELLS: Well, it's certainly a crucial issue for Bush, because as a man who has a limited understanding of the world beyond the American electorate, he's dependent on his seconds, on advisers like Cheney and Condoleezza Rice. His close foreign policy advisers—Rumsfeld, Wolfowitz and Perle are the other principal ones—represent the hard core of the neoconservative movement and are proponents of the totally new direction in American policy that preventive intervention represents. Men of the right and men who are absolutely convinced that America is under a threat, a great threat. So it's no longer an issue of whether we have clients or satellites, it's simply that the United States is going to do whatever it feels it must to protect itself. The US and the US alone is going to determine the policy that best protects American interests. It's not going to worry very long about the opinion of allies, or seek multipolar solutions.

The Cold War model is no longer valid in thinking of America's relations with the rest of the world. Instead, the

American administration is looking to another model—a model that works under terrorist threat. And the only models there are the UK, to a small extent, in dealing with the IRA, but the better model is Israel. And the fact that so many of Bush's closest counselors are Jewish is no doubt a factor in this. But post 9/11, Bush too has a deep appreciation for Israel's situation—under threat from an irrational hate-filled force—and a respect for the determination of Israel's right wing, in the person of Ariel Sharon, not to give an inch to that threat. That identification was really hardened by what happened in September 2001. All of a sudden the terrorism wasn't just something that you read about being carried out in Jerusalem or in Tel Aviv. It was something that was being carried out in New York and Washington.

And I think there's also been a layer of feeling in the United States that the manifestation of anti-Americanism that followed the action at NATO and at the UN matches up on this particular subject.

You know, we're dealing not just with the reality of what happened, the reality of this clash of world views. We also have to face up to the perception that accompanied the reality, the wreckage that was strewn about after the clash. And part of that wreckage, part of that perception, is that the anti-Americanism in France is just anti-Semitism in disguise. The French don't like American policy because it's a policy that favors Israel, and that if American didn't favor Israel the world would be a simpler, less troubled place. That is another way of re-stating an old and horrifying phenomenon: This wonderful land of The Rights of Man sent thousands of Jews to die in Germany. Not in response to edicts from Berlin, but willfully and resolutely, with assiduity, with a certain pleasure.

COLOMBANI: No. You can't mix anti-Americanism and anti-Semitism. And if it is true that there is uneasiness in the Jewish commnity of France caused by the rise of anti-Semitic acts, the frequency of the incidents here has never reached the level it has in America. Anti-Semitism has unquestionably grown in certain European countries, including France; but it has also grown in the United States. On the other hand, it is also true in France, that there is a standardization in certain areas of anti-Semitic discourse, namely in schools; just as it is also true that anger felt towards the Israeli government, so prevalent among young Muslims, is often redirected towards convenient, nearby, European Jews.

The point which seems clear and yet misunderstood in France, is that American leaders turn to Israel, as led today by Ariel Sharon, in their search for the anti-terrorist model. From this point of view, the French perception—which is shared by French leaders, seems to me to be the following. First: The French underestimate the psychological and patriotic impact of the events of September 11 in the United States. Second: The right wing governing the United States is not perceived as "neoconservative," but rather as "reactionary," as a hard, religious right wing bordering on fundamentalism. It is reputedly allied with the Israeli right, influenced by it, and for starters, also rejects the creation of a Palestinian state elsewhere than in Jordan. Hence, criticism of the American right wing and criticism of the Israeli right wing are intermingled. This is the vision that Hubert Vedrine shares—which is the same vision at the Quai d'Orsay[7] of yesterday and today. The idea of a reactionary right in the United States is also Jacques Chirac's dream, and in many aspects of internal politics, the Chirac right wing faction doesn't hesitate to follow the lead of the American right.

Last, but not least, about Vichy: There are enough reasons to worry about the state of our relations without bringing that into consideration. Yes, the French government commited crimes, which Chirac admitted in a speech commemorating the roundup at the Vel d'Hiv,[8] a particularly odious episode in the annals of the

French Police, where they rounded-up men, women and children just because of their Jewish faith and sent them to death camps.[9] But up until the end of 1941, Roosevelt's United States had almost normal relations with Nazi Germany; and Franklin Delano Roosevelt's representatives worked a lot with Vichy, against de Gaulle and the Free French.

Let's avoid a battle of clichés, or the accounting of our mutual, national turpitudes. We had the Dreyfus Affair and the anti-Semitism of the period between the two world wars, but we never had the equivalent of Ivy League colleges in France.[10]

It is disastrous to see the American media reason this way. Let's avoid turning legitimate American anxiety into anti-French imprecations.

WELLS: Bush is a man who, as we say, doesn't take prisoners. He is naturally decisive, being decisive is important to the way he wants the electorate to see him. Once he makes up his mind, it's important for him to move ahead. When he has made a decision, he wants to see it carried out. There's no room for doubt, there's no room to express doubt about the course of action the president has decided on.

How politically could he have allowed any doubt after dumping Osama bin Laden and Saddam Hussein into the same basket? Why, the electorate wouldn't have waited to slaughter him. Not at the polls, but in the polls. His approval rating would have been at 20 percent, rather than 80 percent.

The very haunted vision that he had, and that he was able to sell to the voters, was that America was a victim of the same kind of terrorism as Israel, carried out by products of the same hothouse. And ripe for being dealt with by American power and American exceptionalism. In Iraq as in Afghanistan, it was time for America to stand and deliver.

Was there another element that was more deeply personal? The aspect of finishing the job that Bush the 41st (together with

Cheney and Powell) had failed to finish a decade earlier? Probably, yes. But again, with respect to Freud and Jung and Dr. Joyce Brothers, I'll not go there.

I also do not know whether—having failed to dispense with Osama bin Laden—there was a knowing, calculated political decision to convert the war on terrorism into a war against Saddam Hussein. I don't make that judgment—if post-war operations in Iraq continue to go badly, and if Osama bin Laden stays on the loose, Bush will certainly hear that accusation in the course of the election campaign in 2004. In fact, he's already hearing it, and his numbers in the polls are slipping significantly. I would posit only that Bush saw them as products of the same incubator, and as vectors of the same kind of violence against innocents.

COLOMBANI: To get back to the question of the president's entourage, in the eyes of the French, Dick Cheney is an example of the worst that America has to offer—a mixture of public and private interests. America wages war to make profit for companies in which Dick Cheney has been a stockholder, owner, adviser, lawyer. Dick Cheney represents the dark side of Bush. What a contrast with George Bush the father and his advisor Brent Scowcroft, who were appreciated, respected and listened to in France as well as all over Europe. George Bush Jr., his entourage, and especially Dick Cheney, are caricatures in comparison. Condoleezza Rice made her reputation in Europe by declaring, "Forgive the Russians, ignore the Germans, punish the French!" There is no doubt that her mission is to make Russia a privileged ally; the key element in a scenario which is unfavorable to the European Union, where Russia serves as trump card in a new anti-European hand. Hence Rice, whose specialty is Russia, is seen as one of the authors of this plan designed to prevent a Franco-German Europe. Beyond that, the hawks, the Richard Perles, Paul Wolfowitz, Cheney, Rice, are viewed as a horde of savages, who play the universe like a

Western, trigger-happy and dividing the spoils of war (oil, Public Works…), like Indian lands in years past.

On the French side, it's the Chirac-Villepin duo which dominates. In this couple, neither one restrains the other. At this point in time, Chirac would have fared better with a mind less unbridled, colder than Dominique de Villepin, perhaps someone like Alain Juppé. Alain Juppé has a rational mind, and might have been able to play the role of moderator to Jacques Chirac. Without prejudging the future of the Chirac-Villepin relationship, which in my opinion is not going to last, Villepin is to Chirac what Chirac was to Georges Pompidou for a while: a member of the cavalry. The problem is that Chirac has remained a "hussar," the soldier who executes the most difficult charge, right behind enemy lines, sword drawn. Villepin adds flamboyance, a certain brilliance. But neither one, nor the other (perhaps the latter will become one someday) are strategists. Villepin is Chateaubriand, a poet-writer, performing a complex role today. How can he contain the uninterrupted flow of his thoughts, sometimes chaotic, sometimes dazzling? Who else now? Chateaubriand wasn't a great minister of foreign affairs, but he was a great poet. Contrary to what is generally believed in France, one doesn't have to be a man of letters to become a good minister. Villepin encompasses two visions: the twilight of a world coming apart and the wonderfully utopic exhilaration of a world to come. Except that given his position within the 5th Republic— which is a regime constructed around and for its president—the Foreign Minister is responsible for inventing strategy, tactics, negotiation, patience. Paired with a president who might become irate over an ill-used sentence, word or other form of annoyance, the team could cause great damage. An example was when Chirac berated the countries newly come to the European Union because of their lesser-European attitude towards the Iraq issue. While an advantageous position for internal politics, it was disastrous on the foreign front, and contributed to France's isolation.

Perhaps the Chirac-Villepin duo is not best equipped to deal with the behavior of those whom most of the EU views as a horde of savages.

WELLS: "O wad some Power the giftie gie us
  To see oursel's as ithers see us!"[11]

A band of savages? These the leaders of the Free World?

Well, there is the caricature of Cheney, moving between the highest echelons of government to business and back to government again. But I don't know that condemning him as a savage offers more than the temporary satisfaction of scoring a point for your debate team.

I would not argue that there is no *noyau dur*[12] in America, and particularly in the Republican Party. Big business looks out for itself, with a conviction that business makes the economy strong, and a strong economy benefits everyone.

There is a different kind of *noyau dur* here in France, I think, and it too is quite protective of itself. It moves between government and the big enterprises that government owns, and it serves a sclerotic, noncompetitive system that has to be propped up with one of the highest rates of taxation in Europe. We French taxpayers are still paying off the Credit Lyonnais[13] scandal. And for Elf, where it is highly developed, a well-groomed symbiosis between government and government enterprise served corruption at the highest levels. What good about the French system did that represent?

Nearly half a century ago a member of the Eisenhower Cabinet, Defense Secretary Charles Wilson, was pilloried before American public opinion for saying: "What's good for General Motors is good for America." It wasn't a politic thing to say, since he had run that corporate giant, but it was fundamentally true. There is a concept, not limited to America, of doing well by doing good, of profiting financially from actions that nobly serve the public good. Out of respect for your argument, I will grant that Cheney stands to benefit financially from the war. "What's good for Iraq is good for Halliburton," to paraphrase Charlie Wilson, and good for Cheney's portfolio. But as improbable as you no doubt find it, it's unlikely that Cheney's financial well-being was a factor at any level, including Cheney's own level, in any of the decision making about Iraq. And don't forget that whatever there is in his portfolio is hidden, it's in a blind trust administered by someone else.

Look: There is enormous concern among these "savages" about American security because there is an enormous concern among the American people. Is that hysterical? That depends, doesn't it, on what target is hit next.

In parallel with that concern, there is a deep bewilderment over why there's no appreciation of that anxiety here in Old Europe. We all have the same enemy, and that is international terrorism. We all face the same danger, which can only be considered imminent. Richard Reid was the last known terrorist to get on an airplane, and that was in Paris. So the threat has to be considered just as great at Roissy as at Logan.

In response to that threat, there is a total, categorical unwillingness by Americans to tolerate it and there is a perception in the US that Europeans are too willing to accommodate terrorists. That's unfair, I know. There have been more arrests of terrorists, more plots averted here in France than in the United States or anywhere else. But we're not dealing with fairness, but with perception—as well as how those perceptions are used to influence the electorate.

I have nothing to add to your brilliant characterization of Chirac and Villepin and their relationship. I think that their first real failure in this instance was one of diplomacy, but the overall failure was enormous. They misunderstood American determination, they misunderstood the relationship between the president and his cabinet, and they misunderstood which side Powell would be on. Especially after Villepin betrayed him. Villepin's lack of astuteness cost him more than a friend. It silenced the only point of view of reason within the administration on this issue.

COLOMBANI: In fact, Villepin's mistake with regards to Powell ruined the capital which France might have gained from the quality of the relationship the two men enjoyed previously. The disappointment is even greater in that for France, Powell has always incarnated the European spirit, one of moderation, pacifistic, pacifying, diplomatic, taking allies into account, discussing with them, always worried about creating a consensus. There is no doubt in my mind that part of the French-American divorce was caused by the break in relations between Powell and Villepin. Let's not put too much blame on the French Minister's side. What Powell took for a personal affront was perhaps the best way for him to rally to the "hawks" camp, joining those who wanted war without the United Nations. If this episode had not taken place, it would have been infinitely more difficult for Americans to talk about French "betrayal." In fact, up until the month of December 2002, the two nations individually seemed to perform a division of roles which was more or less explicit. France had maintained that the United States accept "half" the French approach, to split the difference: First, pass a resolution, in principle reinforcing UN inspections in Iraq. Then and only then, if progress was made, armed intervention would ensue. All went well up until the vote on the first resolution. Then, along came the crisis. The French interpretaton is that Powell defended his point of view. But as the Secretary of State is a former military man, and as his point of view was not retained, he felt he should defer to his president's decision. It was important for Powell to make his point of view heard, but he would certainly not resign if Bush's opinion was not the same as his. Disappointment in France stemmed from an erroneous analysis in which the British may have participated. Villepin thought that Powell would go from push to shove with Bush, as Powell wanted a calendar and a plan of action controlled by the UN. As soon as it became apparent that the United States felt that the first resolution was merely a concession to their allies to allow them to join the coalition and nothing more, Villepin and Chirac chose to veto. And they believed that Powell had surrendered. On the contrary, Powell might have felt betrayed by Villepin on that famous day, January 20. Personnally, before January 20, the contacts that I had told me with certainty that the operations calendar was "set" for mid-March. Before that, a source told me, Chirac would have difficulty winning over French public opinion. My sources led me clearly to believe that Chirac had promised, one way or another, to participate. What did the French do next? On January 20, they called a meeting on terrorism which Powell did not want to attend because the United States commemorates Martin Luther King Jr. on that date. Villepin insisted, invoking their budding friendship. Powell showed up. At the end of the meeting, throughout which Villepin abstained from speaking about Iraq, proving that Iraq was not the only topic on the planet's agenda—the French minister addressed the press, rejecting the "adventure" and the "military shortcut" which "our American friends" proposed. Powell was furious, spoke of a "diplomatic ambush" and felt personally betrayed. In the history of our relations, there is now a before and an after January 20, 2003.

WELLS: It's absolutely right that there was a rupture between the two men, and it carried personal overtones. There was also a matter of timing, because Jan. 20 was Martin Luther King Day in the US. For Powell, that was not just another holiday and certainly not a day off from work. There was enormous symbolism because of the day itself, and many people have pointed out the worthwhile calls on his time because of the holiday that Powell had to turn down in order to respond to Villepin's insistence that he come to the UN for a debate on terrorism.

Then once there, the night before this debate, Villepin surprises him—we would say "sandbags" him—by laying out this hard new French position on Resolution 1441. That was bad diplomacy.

And misreading the intent of the administration, and Powell's fragile position within the administration, was a casebook study in failed statecraft.

COLOMBANI: France had accepted a program which included two resolutions, which it had originally proposed and then turned its back on when it became clear the United States had planned the war for March 15 and that the war barely included the United Nations, if at all. A few days after January 20, Colin Powell went to the World Economic Forum at Davos, which this year did not focus on the economy per usual, but concentrated on the growing anxiety in the business world provoked by the perspective of war in Iraq. Speaking to the press, the Secretary of State explained that in his opinion, the French had no way of knowing that the second resolution would legitimize the war.

But despite maneuvers and countermaneuvers on both sides, you have to admit that we were witnessing the confrontation of two visions of the future.

WELLS: Yes, two visions, which have long been merely separate, but now seem to be through opposite ends of the telescope.

COLOMBANI: France is not the only country to have a different view of the universe than the Bush administration. In all Italian villages, balconies were covered with multicolored banners on which were written the word "peace." The Italians demonstrated for peace, showing profound rejection of the way in which war had been declared. In France, there were few demonstrations, little agitation, no deep movement. It is also true that the official line, of both the government and the opposition, was to avoid demonstrating. It seems to me that the mistake was to imagine that one may make a distinction between the pro-American Europeans and the anti-American French. The Spanish, Italian, Greek, German, Belgian and even British opinions were at least hostile, and at most reticent.

There was on the other hand, in France and elsewhere in Europe, the denunciation of a war begun in conditions that were globally unacceptable and poorly prepared. The ensuing events proved that the European plan devised mainly by France, which consisted in only fighting under the United Nations flag in order to mobilize a major UN presence, a UN administration, a UN banner, was infinitely preferable to the Americans fighting the battle alone.

The prestige that Clinton enjoyed in France and all over Europe in fact, was real. His legal misadventures were clearly perceived as part of a political plot. We might believe that he would have had a more multilateral attitude. On the other hand, anti-Bushism today feeds anti-Americanism and is allowing Clinton to make a comeback. Let's not forget that for the French as well as Europeans, Bush holds the record for capital punishment. Besides which, Bush is perceived as the winner of a fixed vote, holding a minority in his country. He didn't win the popular vote, but won on a technicality. He latched onto the presidency and is the former governor of Texas. Sentiment against the death penalty is strong in Europe and is a cultural marker. To what may we compare Bush? To Chinese leaders, leaders in Iran? In addition, the period following September 11, one of instant, spontaneous solidarity, could have been the sign of America turning to its allies, rather than turning away from them. In six months, he squandered this capital with operations in Iraq and lent credit to the idea—without doubt a false interpretation of the American point of view—that September 11 and the campaign following in Afghanistan were only a parenthesis. Once that shock-wave past, we went back to square one in the Bush White House whose priority was Saddam Hussein. At least that's what we thought. Which does not mean that there was only sweetness and light on the side of the French in this business.

And now from America, we feel a true, powerful anti-French movement. No other example comes to mind, than Australia in the 60s and 70s, which was a very anti-French period. Memories persist: of the British conquest of the French fleets in Australia and New Zealand; of the ever-present reminder that France was a nuclear power in the Pacific Ocean; a horrible colonizer in New Caledonia and French Polynesia. Such Francophobic ambiance was reinforced by nuclear tests in the coral reefs at Mururoa and by the French leaving the military command of NATO in 1966. But in comparison to what has flown in the United States against the "F" country, that seems moderate. The theme of the "surrender monkey" is both grotesque and obviously counterproductive. Must I insist that saying no to war does not mean that, ipso facto, we stop being allies? The United States said no to war in Algeria, but we didn't stop being allies. The United States disapproved and forced France and Great Britain to interrupt the expedition in Suez, but that did not result in a major break.

WELLS: The recent wave of Francophobia in the United States is bigger than anything I've witnessed before. But I have to say its basis has been there all along, incipient or inchoate, but present.

The roots of America's Francophobia are as deep as our republic is old. At the same time that Thomas Jefferson and Benjamin Franklin were expressing admiration for France, the puritanical John Adams was condemning French decadence and licentiousness. In the last century, for everyone who said "Paris is where good Americans go when they die," there were a hundred who felt disrespected by the French and disrespect for this wonderful nation. In *The Music Man*, revealing that Marian the Librarian read Balzac was enough to reveal also just how deep the trouble was right there in River City. I'm afraid that "How you gonna keep 'em down on the farm after they've seen Paree"[14] was not about the freedom our Doughboys would find in their overseas expedition, but rather about the licentiousness.

More recently, my own knowledge of this particular variation on us and them, the way "we" feel about "you," is post-war. It relates specifically to the animosity that de Gaulle demonstrated toward the United States. He had found no friend in the US, no trustworthy ally, even. And it wasn't that long after the war, less than a generation, that he pulled France out of NATO, flaunted his nuclear independence and flirted with the Soviet Union. Even before that he expressed suspicion of Lend-Lease and the Marshall Plan, which after the Normandy invasion probably constituted America's finest hour. "Lately God has taken to thinking of himself as de Gaulle" was the punch line of a joke I liked to tell in the 1960s. Which of course reflects the same sentiments that Roosevelt expressed 20 years earlier, which had led to de Gaulle's distaste and distrust for America.

So for us it all boils down to a resentment and a reaction "after all we've done for you." We have never been enemies, we like to say (aside from an obscure series of naval encounters in the 18th century), but we have never really been friends either. Lafayette's and Rochambeau's valiant contributions to American independence were swept away in the furor that led to the Alien and Sedition Act. Pershing's valor was forgotten in Vichy.

And now, there you are again. Being contrary, challenging American exceptionalism, refusing to acknowledge that we alone "stand for peaceful relations among nations." I speak in irony there, but in irony sometimes we stumble upon the regrettable truth.

Analysis often consists of what you see in yourself, and something I know about myself is that compared with this wonderful, sophisticated country, I am an upstart. Our history is that of an upstart nation, of people who have fled (my own forebears, some of them, fled France after the revocation of the Edict of Nantes). We fled oppression, whether political or economic, we're proud of having made our own way, and as a people and a nation we reinforce that in successive waves of immigration, reinforcing our hardy, uncultured stock. As we look back toward old, aristocratic Europe, there is a fair amount of suspicion and insecurity. Those reactions are particularly strong, I think, toward the French, "the only thing wrong with France." It was not so long ago that the French government tourist agency gave lessons in being polite to Americans. Over 24 years, the question I invariably get when I tell Americans I live in France is, "How do you put up with the snottiness?" Of course, that's not true. I travel across France all the time and I know it's not true. Less true here in fact than in New York. But among my countrymen, only 18 percent of whom have passports, that's the take on the French.

There is a general suspicion of foreigners in the United States, particularly foreigners who push back, the way the French do in policy and the Japanese more so in business.

But France truly is a special case. And it's because you hold yourself as special. There's no "going along to get along" with France. And there is no other example that I can think of, of a country that's an ally and a friend that says "no" more than it says "yes."

So when you talk about this phenomenon in the United States being rare, it's really not rare. It's always been there, repressed maybe but not even under the surface.

As you point out, it's quite puzzling: There are German officials who made patently anti-American remarks during the campaign. And the comparison of Bush to Hitler was way beyond acceptable discourse. (Like a recent identification I saw in *Newsweek* of Chirac and Saddam. Beyond the pale.)

But there were no similar public comments in France. And yet Germany has escaped the virulence that has been heaped on France. Germany has not been the target of this phobia, because this was one incident, it wasn't part of a long history of disagreement between two peoples. And the fact that is does have so much currency now is one of the things that makes me think that it's there for a long time. It's not something that's going to go away easily.

We've talked about it in terms of the press. It's not just the right-wing press. The *Washington Post* itself which is thought to be liberal but is really center right in its editorial positions, has been particularly critical of France over Iraq. Many of The *Post*'s columnists—notably Charles Krauthammer and George Will—have been very, very critical of France. Even at the New York *Times*, which is unquestionably liberal, Thomas Friedman proposed that France lose its seat on the Security Council, because it wasn't worthy of that position.

I have compared it to a disease, a virus like SARS. It crops up, then it breaks out, and it infects a whole race. All of a sudden everybody has the same symptoms, which are that it's not just OK to bash France but you're supposed to bash France. I do think of it as a disease, which racism is.

COLOMBANI: Yes. The word out in the press was to "kick France in the behind" for having forgotten D-Day. What is most surprising, as seen from France, is the extent to which the press takes the official viewpoint, of the leaders, accepting their bad arguments, without distancing themselves, lacking critical spirit or at least showing very little. This is a discovery for French opinion which tended to put the "Anglo-Saxon" press on a pedestal. There is not one French person having visited the United States recently—and they are many— who has not been impressed by the drama shown on television, as if Francophobia was the new anti-Communism, with the traditional accusations, light years away from normal journalistic coverage. This discovery of a media which is globally very ideological, very militant and all for the good of Bush, makes you think twice about the "American model." From this angle, France has perhaps provided a convenient alibi for internal politics. But such excessive behavior still leaves us perplexed: Bush's target was Saddam—who is next on the list, Chirac?

In fact, all this noise is a sign of the times, times where Washington doesn't even bother taking the necessary precautions to convince governments and regimes to change. Europeans still remember the American ploy to prevent the day of "historic compromise" from coming, when the Christian-Democrats and the Italian Communists sought to merge. And closer to our generation, Chancellor Helmut Kohl's arrival to power in 1982 owed much to American pressures on the liberal allies of the SPD (Sozialdemokratische Partei Deutschlands, or Social Democratic Party) which was then in power in what was still West Germany. Well, from now on and this is the good news, Washington can no longer "punish" a resisting government except through the more democratic pathways of discussion!

This being said, you have to admit that Bush and Powell may have legitimately felt a sort of "betrayal" on a man-to-man level. Knowing Chirac, I can imagine him saying something to Bush along the lines, "In any event, we will be there for you," or using a pat response in conversation which might be construed as a commitment, but which in fact, wasn't really one, as according to an old Chirac adage, "Promises are only real to those who choose to believe them." It still seems impossible to me that at least part of American public opinion does not wake up, react, find its critical sense once again and question an intervention that was badly led and poorly prepared. Even if immediate security needs allowed Bush to mix this up with the war in Iraq, there must come a time when American public opinion considers this oversimplification as abusive and sanctions Bush.

WELLS: It is true that many Americans on the left regard Bush as an international terrorist himself. But the dominant emotion remains one of general insecurity and the prevailing attitude is that the government is dealing with that threat. As for whether Bush abused that attitude, in converting a war on terror into a war against Saddam Hussein, look how long it took American opinion to turn against the war in Vietnam. We all agree now, nearly all of us, that the policies that got us to Vietnam were wrong. But at the time, it took 10 or 15 years from engagement to full disengagement.

The Constitution in essence obliges the president to sell his foreign policy to the voters, but once it's sold, the public's commitment to overseas initiatives is almost part of our national mythology. You don't criticize the administration when it's involved in war. And if the war is wrong—and that may just mean unwinnable, I'm not sure—it takes a long time for realization to take hold. It won't take a decade, as it did in Vietnam, particularly if the current phase of guerrilla warfare continues. The United States is going to have to deal much more effectively with ending the war and rebuilding the country. And it's going to have to deal with it in a way that costs a whole lot less than 4 billion dollars a month and that involves the death of a soldier practically every day. The current situation will have a rapidly wearying and wearing effect on American public opinion.

But one of the paradoxes is, I suspect, that when that happens, there will still be a suspicion and distrust of France. That's unreasonable and it's tribal, but it's part of reality.

COLOMBANI: More often that not, anti-Americanism is an inherited "French passion" rather than an attitude based on reason. However, the times we live in are not anti-American in the traditional sense of the word. For unfortunately, there is a traditional sense. French anti-Americanism is real and powerful. Nevertheless, like Jean Francois Revel,[15] I believe that the anti-American obsession never held a majority in French society. There is no hatred, but persistence and survival of the three currents which nourish or reactivate anti-Americanism.

In the beginning was the far right, in the 30s which spit on democracy and therefore spit on America as the model of that democracy. To this hatred was added the rejection of a technological society.

Next came the anti-Americanism of the Gaullist family, born from the deceptions of the war and Roosevelt's errors. God knows Roosevelt was a great leader, but in France, he did make serious mistakes, which is why his diplomats tried everything but Gaullism. It was as if they marched to the beat, "Anything but de Gaulle!" France owes as much to Churchill as to Eisenhower (who were both popular men), for preserving its identity and allowing it to escape the American executive project of imposing a military government (the AMGOT[16]), with its Paul Bremer of the moment. America already wanted to punish France. America's attitude today is all the more paradoxal in that to speak of Vichy is to forget that Vichy's most important diplomatic support came from the American government. France arising from its ashes was Gaullist and resistant, pushing Vichy out with gut strength. This historical sin was very present in the mind of de Gaulle when he came back to power in 1958. In spite of all that, in 1962 the very same man did not ask to see the photos that Secretary of State Dean Acheson was ready to show him proving that the Russians had installed missiles in Cuba. De Gaulle felt that from the moment Kennedy thought the safety of the United States was threatened, France must commit itself. And it is the same man who, four years later, kicked NATO forces off French soil. France has demonstrated that it is possible to affirm its French identity, or European identity, without missing vital agreements with the United States.

Was the security of the United States the issue in Iraq? Chirac, who undoubtedly nursed from the same breast of that particular Gaullist form of anti-Americanism, thought not. Perhaps he was mistaken. But the deed is done.

Finally, there is the anti-Americanism of the left, coming from the far left. During the entire Cold War, there was good and evil.

The capital of good was Moscow, the evil, Washington. And vice-versa. In the name of this conflict between Moscow and Washington, the Gulag and the Free World, to be perfectly honest, serious events fueled the left's anti-Americanism. The war in Vietnam and the coup d'etat against Allende, to cite only the two best known episodes. Our Greek, Spanish and Portuguese friends know how many long and dark years it took to pay back American support to their military dictators. Not to mention the Argentinian dictators and dirty tricks from the CIA.

In parenthesis, I would add: America has conquered Russia and that's a good thing. But it left the table after the Cold War without settling accounts. At the very moment when all of Eastern Europe was soul-searching, when the famous and deadly KGB was finally obliged to give accounts, for the CIA it was like water off a duck's back. There was never any true self-criticism of McCarthyism, or of the support lent to death squads in Latin America on the pretense of blocking the Communists. There is a museum of horrors of the American Cold War. Had these been confessed at the time, perhaps America would be spared of the temptation today to go back to such deplorable methods.

Therein lies the historical sources of anti-Americanism, to which one might add—at least for part of the public opinion—the turning point of the Reagan years and their European equivalent, Thatcherism, which created yet another cultural gap.

What's left today? For Chirac, reflexes that function like a type of genetic code for part of the French right wing, which is currently in power. The anti-Americanism of the far right is compensated by the admiration that this school of thought holds for the Bush method. The French left or governmental left (since anti-Americanism is part of the very foundation of the far left), is much more American, or as we mentioned previously, more "Atlantic" than the right of this administration because of the Gaullist period, but also because anti-communism and denunciation of the

Soviet regime are located in the origins of the Social-Democrat family. It is not hostile to the United States and can easily identify with the Democratic Party.

On the other hand, the new political frontier today is comprised of movements born from radical criticism of globalization. In France, we say *mondialization* ("worldwide-ism"), which we would like to be different or "other" than globalization. Among other things, globalization is criticized because it translates into American hegemony. In the "worldwide-ism" movement, there is some recycling of the habitual criticism of "American imperialism" by the far left, albeit recalling the advantages that only an American government which still considers itself imperial may offer. There is some new material however, including the strong demand to take the planetary needs for development, social and environmental justice into account, which today concern all rich, developed nations and not just Washington. But if one had to summarize popular opinion today, there is more hatred for Bush, than for America.

And all the more so, as ever since the Liberation, Europe lives in an American sphere. It certainly seeks independence, but division exists between those who feel Europe must build opposite, if not against the United States and those who feel it must build alongside the United States. This discussion is legitimate. It has nothing to do with anti-Americanism.

Ultimately, we are living through a great paradox. The French are perceived as traitors by the United States, while France would like to remain a privileged ally, not on the sidelines.

The same French people who are proud of their "cultural differences" (whereas many of their cultural references are now imported from the United States, i.e. in literature, cinema and even more so in television), participate in the same universe. All of these things contribute to the feeling that Americans are close to us and not absolute strangers.

WELLS: Historical sources are one thing, and hearing such an erudite explanation truly clarifies and contributes to understanding, but perception is another. And there are a lot of things that Americans have perceived as being anti-American, when in fact they are merely anti-globalization, or they are part of a long history of French protectionism. The cultural exception, genetically modified foods, the WTO, McDonald's, all the things that José Bové[17] builds his demagoguery around. Well, we have demagogues too, people who put "freedom fries" on the list they still call a "menu." And even if we didn't, the issues are sufficiently broad and sufficiently complex that they get confused and exploited in America, too. And in the popular mindset, it's, "We pulled their chestnuts out of the fire, and that's all the thanks we get."

Now I happen to think that Churchill was the greatest man of the 20th century. But you only have to remember the Dardanelles[18] to recall his competence as a military strategist. I don't think it diminishes his overwhelming historical stature to say he was a great political leader, not a great military strategist. His strategy in the battle for Europe, you will recall, was to target the "soft underbelly," to invade through Italy so as to assure a post-war role in Eastern Europe for the West and not for Stalin. 350,000 men were killed in the Italian campaign, and the most significant result was to prove the Americans right, that it was necessary to defeat Hitler's armies where they were, in France, Belgium and Germany itself.

It is true that Roosevelt resisted de Gaulle's entreaties—he simply detested the man. He detested his arrogance and his self importance.

In the present context, though, I think the issue isn't Churchill's strategy, or the bad chemistry between Roosevelt and de Gaulle. It's American flesh and blood. Ten thousand Americans died in the first month of the Normandy campaign, and 29,000 in the first three months. An American cannot stand in that cemetery at Utah Beach and not shed tears. The Normandy invasion is as big a factor in the American psyche as all the cowboys who ever rode the range—though perhaps not as big as 9/11 is for today's generation. And the parallel of the French "so what?" reaction to 9/11 shouldn't be lost.

America bore the brunt in '44—American had the bodies, the cannon fodder, because America was bigger. Part of being bigger is being the boss: "I'm in charge here." And the French, often much to their credit, have stood up to that. But that has not always been well received. It's perceived not as a dispute on policy or even an argument among friends, but as an inevitable consequence of anti-Americanism.

COLOMBANI: Perhaps this unilateral perception which you say is massive, comes from the weakness of the left in the United States. Many of the platforms of the far left come from movements which are considered radical. Take for example, anti-globalization. The movement which is in vogue today called ATTAC (Action pour une Taxation des Transactions financiéres por l'Aide aux Citoyens), partially reflects what remains of Communist ideology, with a simplistic plan for the universe, continuing to locate the capital of evil on the side of Washington. The vice president of this movement is an American woman, Susan George. She represents the radical American left and is all too familiar with criticism of the ties between imperialism and the large trust—the trusts that stock the alimentary arms which increase their power. And she is familiar with the ever pertinent criticism of the role certain pharmaceutical giants play in waging war against HIV in Africa. Unfortunately these are no longer best-selling stories in the United States. In fact, if the truth be told, the only thing that the left wing might accomplish today is to help Al Gore lose an election, as its voice is no longer heard.

WELLS: The leadership of America's left is weak because its political base continues to decline. Only 33 percent of the electorate describe themselves as Democrats, in one recent poll. And only 35 percent of the Democrats describe themselves as liberal. I think liberalism has lost out in America because its old ideas failed to deliver its lofty ideals, and now though it has the same ideals, it has no new ideas. The only Democrat to be elected president in the last quarter century, Bill Clinton, did it by taking votes from the center, not because of the strength of the left. On the other hand, the conservative movement is energized, if for no other reason than that the Republicans are the party of national security.

As for the economic scene, I suspect that Europe would risk more fundamental problems if the left were in power because its instincts are protectionist, where as Republicans are fully committed to free trade.

Free trade policies, in the hands of the biggest economies, do bear imperialistic markings. I assume this is what Mitterrand was alluding to when he said that Europe didn't know it yet, but it was engaged in a war with United States. That won't change. We have the same kind of economic base and we're going to fight over markets and over jobs.

COLOMBANI: French-American relations are not only made up of conflicts and competition. Why not recall that France and the United States are two sister republics. The American Constitution was forged in a great moment of French intellectual history. The American Revolution was born from that same moment and after the revolutionary period and the Empire, there were years of close alliance between France and the United States, of which the culminating point was undoubtedly the decisive role Pershing played in the victory of the first World War. At the same time, events currently unfolding lead one to believe that the United States has once again picked up the torch of the French Revolution as if it represents a universal dream. This alliance ruptured under the enormous disappointment caused by the collapse of France in 1940. The French Army was the best in the world, the privileged ally and it turns out to be impotent when up against Hitler's army. Seen from the United States, the true French betrayal occurred in 1940. Along came the British alliance. For the French, there undoubtedly exists deep nostalgia for the days of their privileged alliance with the United States. The republican myth is still hidden somewhere. For a nation like ours where history is still taught, this is important.

We are also experiencing a type of transferral where France is now subscribing to the Wilsonian ideal, just as America turns away from it. Briefly, the ideal, which consists of collective security, is supported by Paris and fought in Washington. We are caught in a double historical distortion which to some, makes the American Republic unrecognizeable.

WELLS: Wilsonianism is a great irony in American history. It is recalled now, as indeed you do here, for the nobility of its purpose. But it's a mistake not to recall also that it was a great failure. Wilson always ceded his noble ambitions to realpolitik. He yielded to the British and the French about making the Germans pay. And he yielded to his own Senate and gave up on achieving ratification of the Treaty of Versailles.

Rather than Wilsonionism, the historical imperatives to remember about America are the Monroe Doctrine[19] and Manifest Destiny.[20] And think not of Wilson, but of Theodore Roosevelt. The Monroe Doctrine established the American Hemisphere as out of bounds for European colonisation. And Manifest Destiny justified the expansion westward to the Pacific. And Roosevelt was the first truly aggressive practitioner of American interventionism.

But both of these concepts now have a virtual application that carries them beyond the hemisphere and beyond the oceans, in both directions. And it was the victory in World War II more than any other single factor that we feel gave us the right to that virtual extension. That was amplified again with the collapse of the Soviet empire, but it was World War II that established primacy.

It's not that America set up colonies, or declared anything off limits or claimed land beyond its shores. But we did claim a realm of sorts that we called a sphere of influence. We also called it the Free World. We offered protection to that realm, guaranteeing its freedom and making it possible for the countries in alliance with us to avoid massive military expenditures and concentrate on their economic well-being. De Gaulle was suspicious of NATO, but France would not live so well today without America's military and economic protection, NATO and the Marshall Plan.

Did we expect some loyalty in return? Yes, for that's what alliances do historically. Did we exact fealty? Apparently not— France is the country that can't say yes, and we haven't attacked yet.

The Soviet Union doesn't exist any more and Moscow is now an ally, sort of. But, believing that we all still face a common enemy, America still throws its weight around, and feels not so much entitled to as obligated to.

Is that Wilsonian? Not as we have come to understand the term. But what Wilson practiced was not the Wilsonianism that Europeans mourn. His idea of the League of Nations was a lot closer to "the white man's burden" than to multilateralism. A multipolar world is what led to the world war that he fought. The idea of re-establishing anything similar would of course have been anathema to Wilson. The democracy he wanted to make the world safe for was American democracy.

Wilson was a Presbyterian, which is divine-right Protestantism. His intention was for the Anglo Saxons to convert the world. It was not at all, not for a second, to subjugate American primacy to veto.

America isn't any more Wilsonian than Wilson himself was. It's more isolationist than anything else. Its basic reactions are isolationist unless it feels threatened. Sometimes the sense of threat may be off base, as in Vietnam. But you have only to recall the reluctance to get involved in the Balkans to understand how isolationist the American preference is. World War II is an even more glaring example. Not until we were attacked did we declare war in return.

Now the Bush administration has moved beyond historical reticence about going to war unless attacked because terrorism is a different kind of war.

2
Grounds for the French-American Rivalry

The recent confrontation between France and the United States over military intervention in Iraq leads us to question the ties that bind both countries and the differences that separate them.

Valéry Giscard d'Estaing and Helmut Kohl, both well-informed politicians, agreed that in spite of the fact that "this is not the first time the transatlantic partnership raises questions on both sides, such brief disagreements never rocked the core of values and common interests that continue to define the Western world."[21]

The American specialist in international relations Philip H. Gordon made the same observation: "Between America and Europe, there are no divergences of interests or fundamental values. And for the United States, European democracies are closer allies than in any other region today and will undoubtedly remain so forever. Even if their tactics differ from time to time, for the most part, Americans and Europeans share the same democratic and liberal aspirations for their societies and the rest of the world. They further the existence of an international system for free commerce and communications, easy access to the energy sources of the world, non-proliferation of arms of mass destruction, prevention of human tragedy and the isolation of a small group of dangerous states which do not respect the rights of man and are hostile to the values and interests of the West."[22]

If democracy, the rights of man, international stability and a market economy are all, hands down, aspirations shared by both nations, the evolution of American and French societies over the course of the last decade reveal an ever-widening gap on subjects equally important as war, peace, solidarity, justice, immigration and religion. Henceforth we must ask: Is it less a matter of shared values than a community of interests sealing Franco-American cooperation and friendship?

COLOMBANI: Other than market law and representative democracy—two givens which are certainly essential—we might want to rethink the leitmotif of "shared values." Take the death penalty for example, on which there is a true difference of opinion. In the European mind it has become a cultural marker, constituting a value system. Proof lies in the banning of the death penalty by the European Convention of Human Rights. Anyone wanting to become European must first conform to that criterion. The death penalty, or rather its constant practice in the United States for a good thirty years now, has progressively contributed to digging a true cultural ditch. In that respect, the United States is closer to China or Iran. This is undoubtedly an easy topic to debate, but we pay greater attention to it, as Europe took a long time to rid itself of that reasoning which is still prevalent in the United States.

Nevertheless, it would be absurd to think that there are only genuine defenders of man's rights in Europe or that there are none at all in the United States. I am willing to believe that defenders of the rights of man in the United States are not insensitive to the fate of the prisoners at Guantanamo. But then again, Guantanamo is considered the negation of America's intentions, as it claims to be fighting for democratic principles. Guantanamo is the opposite example. Absence of justice, purely military control, people who have been locked up for almost two years now without trial, some prisoners being released as they have no evidence against them; without doubt, they will be sworn enemies of the United States in the future. Nuremberg was due process of law and internationally recognized as such. From a European point of view, Guantanamo is completely incomprehensible.

Before that, in terms of values, in the 80s we lived through a period of profound disagreement with the United States of the Ronald Reagan years. His idea of replacing the "New Deal" with a "conservative revolution" seemed already reactionary. In any event, his program of social regression contributed to a wider rift with the United States. Today it represents the dominating dogma, whereas after the Second World War, America's victory over the Nazis was the basis for a welfare state. Then came Kennedy's "Great Society" and Johnson's "war against poverty," which were closer to European values. In any case, with the exception of Thatcherism in Great Britain, Europe did not share this experience, which for the middle classes constituted an unquestionable step backwards.

Let's recall that Roosevelt knew how to embody the fundamental values which we have always had in common, before yesterday's Cold War and today's battle against terrorism make those values dissipate; before we are forced to create unnatural alliances in the name of the fight against the Communism of yesteryear and the fight against "Evil" today; before the Reagans, Bushes, and their counter-revolutions make Wall Street converge once again with Main Street—and before the ideology engendering all of the above overwhelms us.

WELLS: The death penalty is part of the baggage we brought with us from European shores. We just haven't yet inherited the influences that would abolish its use. Maybe this is an instance where a trend will blow the other way, and then the American right will decry the Frenchifying of the US, rather than editorialists here decrying the Americanization of France.

I think it's worth noting that the death penalty is practiced in other places than America, at least one of them a center of high culture and an advanced esthetic—I speak of Japan. And yet there is far less discussion of that, no raucous opposition to its use there, and perhaps that is because you expect more of America. That may be fair. In those other countries that still execute criminals—others in Asia, Russia and the other countries of the old Soviet Union, Africa and the Arab countries, South America—I think it's fair to say that the death penalty is part of a cultural heritage. In our own case, too, the death penalty is part of a cultural heritage, the Judeo-Christian heritage, because religion forms the basis for our approach to crime and punishment.

However, you'll not hear me offer a defense of the death penalty. Its continued use in my country is anathema to me, especially after all the recent evidence that it has been misapplied so often. That we still use it—in 38 states, I believe, and by the Federal government too—does constitute a cultural marker. There was a period in which the United States was not applying the death penalty, in which the Supreme Court had effectively put it in suspension. Paradoxically, the consequence of that suspension was a new rush to execute. A number of states adopted laws that met the Supreme Court requirements for constitutionality. And so we went from 0 executions in 1968 to 600 in the last two decades of the century.[23]

You don't have to accept it to try to understand it, and understanding it is clearer when you remember the zealous Protestantism that led to our founding, and the reach of conservative Christianity now. Religion has always played an important role in criminal justice, and supporters of the death penalty quote the Scriptures to justify their beliefs.

For all those reasons capital punishment is not a magic wand issue—meaning that it will take far more than a wave of the hand to reverse the policy. It is, in fact, what's known as a "third-rail" issue in America. If a candidate touches it, it's he who will be electrocuted, put to political death, and not the policy. We recall that Texas executed a lot of people while Bush was governor. But do you remember also that Clinton returned to Arkansas to be present when someone was executed? He left the campaign for the presidency to go back to Little Rock as a symbol of his support for capital punishment.

So it will take a considerable amount of leadership by all possible forces—the president, the Congress, religious leaders, and the popular media, meaning TV and the movies, before there will be a groundswell of opinion to change the law. I think actually that that is beginning to happen. Why? Because fundamentally Americans are fair minded. Once the unfairness of capital punishment is demonstrated—as in Illinois—opposition will build and finally the practice will be abolished.

The moral high ground that the French hold on this issue was seized not all that long ago, only twenty-some years. And I believe that France was one of the last European countries to abolish capital punishment—and the guillotine was every bit as gruesome as electrocution.

As for the denial of human rights for those held at Guantanamo, quite obviously America's Defense and Justice Departments are not respecting the Constitution, or such basic tenets of Common Law as habeas corpus. But the government's first obligation is to protect the nation from the risk of imminent terrorist attack. That has put the country on a war footing, and it has taken prisoners in that war. After it's over, we'll look back and regret and condemn the excesses, as we did after World War II, when Japanese residents in the United States were interned and their property seized. We'll condemn and deplore. But for the time being, most Americans would not accept seeing these prisoners released until it's certain that there are no terrorists among them. It's a sort of internal *realpolitik*.

There's an old truism: First you get strong, and then you get moral. America feels weak in the face of terrorism, and is trying to get strong. Is that approach hypocritical? Well, is any Western democracy free of hypocrisy? I don't remember a vote by the nations of the South Pacific over those unnecessary nuclear tests when Chirac moved into the Élysées Palace. Nor do I remember very much except temporizing from the prime minister about why France sent its agents to New Zealand to sink a peace activist vessel, the Rainbow Warrior.

Many things about America are paradoxical. Our foreign policy, like anyone's foreign policy, is based on self-interest, but that self-interest is often disguised as something noble and altruistic. You have held up the ideals of the noble savage, and you don't see much there but savagery. Well, name for me a country that has an effective foreign policy that has been more beneficial not just for itself, but for its allies?

But on the issues of the death penalty, and habeas corpus, while both are major in terms of abrogating human rights, and our disagreements are fundamental, neither is a strategic issue. American practice can be rightly deplored, but neither the death penalty nor the military trials of the Guantanamo detainees are behavior that would lead to diplomatic rupture. Not even with the UK or Australia, which have nationals being held there. Perhaps because in both of those countries, as in the United States, there is a recognition that an overemphasis on civil liberties misses the nature of the terrorist threat.

But to come back to the question of shared values, and not just the things that divide us, the list of those values is long, and it begins with freedom, just as the relationship between our countries was first cemented in freedom and a revolution to obtain it. The list moves on quickly to a sense of justice, and if we don't have the same method of trying to obtain justice, neither you nor I could say there is no justice in this land or that one. Americans thought it was inadmissible that France balked at extraditing Ira Einhorn, an American who had been convicted of murder, and a particularly gruesome one. For the French, it was inadmissible to send him back to face the death penalty. So there was an accommodation. You perceive our system as distorted by money, and we see yours as distorted by favoritism, by clubbiness. Was justice served by penalizing an underling in the blood scandal,[24] but letting his bosses off the hook? What was just about allowing Paul Touvier to remain at large all those years, or protecting Maurice Papon for 50 years and giving him his freedom after being convicted?[25]

COLOMBANI: This is not a tennis match and we don't have to look into the secret recesses of the closets where we store our respective histories. Let's stick to the topic of common values. We have seen in the United States, as in Europe generally and France in particular, the advent of populist and conservative reactions against humanitarianism and multilateralism from the outside and from guilt about the treatment of minorities and loose morals during the Clinton era, on the inside. But France knows all about this, as witnessed by the last horrible presidential election on April 21, 2002, where during the first round, the candidate from the far right, Jean-Marie Le Pen qualified for the second vote. And as I said, these currents exist in Europe and sometimes even rise to the executive level. But their victory in the United States, reinforced by a neo-imperial tendency, is not a factor that aids in the understanding between the United States and France.

Moreover, as you have said, we have different views on law. How can I explain it? By the disparity of power, as Robert Kagan[26] sees it? Kagan brings to light a danger menacing Europe, of becoming an over-enlarged Switzerland, a community of nations attempting to live free from external threats. Switzerland waited until 2002 to join the United Nations! The same tendency exists in the Scandinavian countries, like Sweden, but also in Germany. The French, on the other hand, are for a "strong Europe." But who believes in that?

In fact, the French and the Americans have one thing in common: They invent a new doctrine for each new situation. Yesterday, the United States was pushing the United Nations and de Gaulle's France refused to recognize an organization with international jurisdiction. Today, the imperial discourse comes from Bush: Chirac believes that only respect for law legitimizes the use of force and insists that the Security Council alone can confirm this. Hence today, France maintains that the only legal war is one condoned by the Security Council, whereas for a long time, it took the opposite stand. The moral of the story is if you are weak, it's better to give in to negotiation and legality. Which raises another question: how important are the values you extol? In Bosnia, Kosovo, the Europeans felt that the defense of certain values—against ethnic cleansing—had to be imposed, by force if necessary. The same values (I'm thinking about Chirac) do not apply in the case of Iraq. Obviously Chirac was against a regime change in Iraq, even if he did want them disarmed.

To get back to law and what one can do with it, one suspects Europe (this is Robert Kagan's famous thesis) of only using it to the extent that it is absolutely necessary, as it only wants to emulate Switzerland anyway. If this were the case, it would bring about the inevitable downfall of Europe. On the other hand, for the United States to feel above the law in the use of force, is the United States adhering to an imperial logic? An empire knows no other law than the use of violence in order to insure its monopoly. This is the beginning of the end of the empire. To use a Napoleonic comparison, his major strategic error was to revert to pre-emptive war. It was pre-emptive war against Spain and Russia that caused Napoleon to lose the French empire. If France had wanted to be a "benevolent" empire, it would have had to create balance in Europe, to concede to its enemies, to invent a multipolar Europe. Today, the United States should be capable of inventing an international system of checks and balances, a balance of strengths, otherwise they are going to get stuck in the mud.

WELLS: It wasn't all that long ago that we were talking about *The End of History*, which was the book of that particular moment. That theory, expounded by Francis Fukuyama, argued that an evolution away from leftist, totalitarian forces had been successfully led by the enlightenment of democratic capitalism. Or perhaps it was the creature comforts available under capitalistic government that led the evolution, because after all, creature comfort had an awful lot to do with the abandonment of Communism. Capitalism actually created wealth, rather than destroying it, so it worked better for the people than Marxism and made their lives better. Recalling *The End of History*, I wonder if Kagan's might not be another "book of the moment"—or idea of the moment, because it began as a treatise, not as a book.

That's immaterial I suppose, because whether it is or not, I think that there's been more discussion based on misunderstanding than of the book itself. The book is usually discussed in France as another example of hateful, anti-European propaganda. And no one quotes Kagan when he writes: "The new Europe is indeed a blessed miracle and a reason for enormous celebration—on both sides of the Atlantic... something to be cherished and guarded, not least by Americans, who have shed blood on Europe's soil and would shed more should the new Europe ever fail."

Personally, I find Kagan's explanations very sound and well documented. But there are several aspects about his arguments that have less to do with their astuteness and more to do with their timing. The first of those is that Kagan is seen as providing validation for the policies of pre-emptive intervention of the Bush administration. The second is that Kagan has understood something and expressed it in accessible ways before anyone else. And that is not that Europe is powerless, which isn't a new concept. Don't forget that (as Kagan points out) Franklin D. Roosevelt thought it was necessary to render Europe powerless after World War II, because Europe's power politics had always ended in disaster and had cost so many American lives. And de Gaulle's intention was not to let that happen.

Franklin D. Roosevelt was dead by the end of the war, but the idea wasn't. And whether or not it motivated Truman as he led the creation of NATO, that alliance removed from Europe a need for individual state power. Did the American umbrella turn Europe into Switzerland? I don't think that comparison bears up. Switzerland removed itself from the application of all kinds of power. Switzerland doesn't want to be noticed. That's clearly not true of France or the UK or Germany. But do those countries have an independent military policy? Separately or together, can they even afford one?

What Kagan has clarified is just how much America has changed and how much the world has changed. And that has enabled an understanding not just that the US is unfettered by its Cold War fears and obligations, but more importantly, that it has the strength to act alone if it deems that necessary. The United States is the only militarily empowered force that can deal with a threat like global terrorism, which is far more dangerous than the risk of another war in Europe. And of course since the US itself has been attacked in this new warfare, it has been willing to attack in return, and to attack pre-emptively.

It's not a fear of Soviet tanks that sows panic now, or a nuclear Armageddon—except in the context of the assumption that if Osama bin Laden had had nuclear weapons, he would have used them on 9/11. That sows a great deal of panic. Frankly, the US needs allies in that fight, not just solidarity in its grief.

Where I think Kagan can be faulted is in focusing only on military power and ignoring other kinds. Namely, the power of influence. Which is what Europe wielded as the pivotal force between the United States and the Soviet Union, for instance, and what France wields through the UN. That kind of soft power should not be dismissed. The context for influential maneuvering will change, but not its role and not its usefulness. It was soft power that Bush I appealed to when he created the coalition in the first Gulf War. It was Chirac's withholding of soft power that prevented a real coalition in Iraq and triggered the crisis between our two governments.

But one thing about soft power may be the old truism most often used in another field of basic human behavior: "Use it or lose it." Except I would say: "Use it wisely, or see it wither." I think that the failure of diplomacy resulted in a poor use of soft power on 1441, and now France is struggling to reclaim it. The specter of terrorism actually makes this a far more Hobbesian[27] world than the Soviet threat did. In such a risky world—again, I quote Kagan—the ability to project military "power is the ultimate determinant of security and success."

It's worth pointing out that Kagan also recalls the ancient concept of *raison d'état*, not at all as a justification for any of America's actions but rather to differentiate them from traditional power politics, the power politics practiced by European countries until World War II changed everything. But could you not argue that we heard a contemporary version of *raison d'état* in the petulant scolding that Chirac gave the new East European members of the EU? *"L'Union Européen, c'est moi."* It seems to me that that was the sort of abusive insult that will sting a lot longer than Rumsfeld's snide dismissiveness of "Old Europe." I've had occasion recently to talk with ambassadors from European countries, both East and West, who talk about France in the same tones that are implicit when France talks about the United States. France wants its leadership recognized in Europe and it doesn't want its leadership to be challenged. That is the way the world works, the way it probably always will work.

COLOMBANI: Yes. But that's another subject. It is true that France does not know how to regain the leadership in Europe that it lost after François Mitterrand. It would be more accurate to speak of co-leadership between France and Germany, first under Giscard-Schmitt, then Kohl-Mitterrand.

And it is also true that Jacques Chirac did not embark on the road to conquering Europe and instead—even before the Iraqi affair—he isolated France, namely at the European Summit in Nice. This leads us to the empire: The two basic imperial practices are violence or force, which must be monopolized, and division. Divide and rule. Bush tries to divide Europe to better control it. And foolishly, Chirac encourages him by lecturing the former Eastern bloc countries, the very ones which Washington wants to remove from Franco-German influence. What a mistake!

Let's go back to our basic divergences.

On a democratic level especially, many things differentiate France and the United States. To begin with: General Washington was not General Bonaparte! Forgive my pedantry. But the former became president and gave up power. The latter didn't want to do that. From that moment on their destinies were different. It was the period under Napoleon that structured France, which still lives with this heritage today, namely in terms of centralization and its institutions, whereas those forged by de Gaulle are essentially consular. It is often said that France is monarchic, but it is still Napoleonic.

In the United States, the philosophy is almost the exact opposite. Powers are separated and in principle, balanced.

But comparing our respective models by idealizing one and trashing the other, and vice versa, is a waste of time. Especially since progressively, we all seem to be on the verge of becoming citizens under American law. In business law for example, a system of Anglo-American inspiration conflicts with the European system. Generally speaking, we are all wed to democratic opinion, without being able to clearly define its operative principles, as opposed to the definition of representative democracy presented by Montesquieu and the philosophers of the

Enlightenment. That brings us closer together also. Even if our judicial systems—inquisitorial in France, contrary to the United States—continue to separate us by proposing different concepts of the rights of man as opposed to the State. The Americanization of our laws is seen as the last step in the integration of Europe into the Americanosphere. Henceforth in the name of rejecting the empire.

In fact, these two democracies have rules which are becoming increasingly similar: those governing public life, the means for expressing democratic opinion, criteria for selection of leaders, party life, transformation of European political parties which already are ideological machines, tending towards becoming mere instruments for selecting candidates, as in the United States. But I wonder. This movement seemed irresistible. However we seem to be at a time where opinion is reverting to the past, albeit with some confusion—or perhaps turning violently to the future—when faced with the homogenization of both sides of the Atlantic.

WELLS: Is it just on the two sides of the Atlantic that the homogenization is being felt? I ask that because I think it already extends farther and will extend farther still as an inevitable consequence of globalization. It seems to me that we have actually moved into a situation that anticipates not any sort of world government, but supra-national institutions that will impose an international will on many national actions, though probably not easily on military ones. Another way of thinking about it is the international system of checks and balances you mentioned.

Despite this new age of nationalism, it can be argued that a lot of the institutions of government that assure national self-determination have been weakened and in effect replaced. The European Union is the best example of that. So are NAFTA[28] and the WTO. But there are other examples—the Kyoto Accords would be one if the US had signed. The Law of the Sea Treaty would be another, again if the US had signed. The International Court of Justice. (And yes I do realize that most of the examples I cite are also examples of today's mutant American exceptionalism.)

Thus there is an emerging global democracy of opinion—it may be hard to define, but it certainly is coming into existence. Perhaps it started in the marketplace with commercial democracy—casting dollars and euros and drachmas to elect Coca-Cola the world's favorite drink, or McDonald's the world's favorite eatery. It's a paradox—nationalism has rarely been a more noisome force, whether in Montenegro or Corsica,[29] but nations and boundaries are much less important now than they ever were before. For all the violence in Corsica, or ETA's brutal clamor for independence, we really have moved far beyond the concept of the paramount nation, and toward a homogenization if not yet homogeneity.

On the specific issue of the legal system, and the Americanization of business law in Europe (and around the world), there are two factors. One is just language—as English has spread as the lingua franca of business, the approach to business law has followed. A second reason, I like to think, has to do with Anglo-Saxon genius, which isn't art or music, but governance, including the governance of jurisprudence. The basics of English Common Law are adopted for business because the system is based on fair play. Of course, the basics can be distorted and the system can become blatantly unfair, which is the case in some former British colonies as well as the consequence of mixing money and tort law, as in the United States.

COLOMBANI: Let's also take a look at the relationship to the State, in all its components. Both in Europe and France, even if one challenges the idea of an American empire, one cannot ignore the fact that our universe, our lives—and first and foremost our economic lives—are highly influenced by what happens in the United States. Either we try to distinguish ourselves by stating that while we accept a market economy, we don't accept a market society—which is the discourse of the left. Or we try to explain why we are behind the times, why we lack dynamism in comparison to the qualities of the American model, and especially its flexibility. Just look at how easy it is in the United States to fire someone! That's the discourse of the right.

However, rather than examining the ideological or political arenas, you have to look at the relationship to the State. Ideology? Agreed, the American left is not the European left. Agreed, the European left is much more ideological having been influenced by Marxism. But what separates a Tony Blair from a Bill Clinton, or a Bill Clinton from a Schröeder, or a Schröeder from a French socialist is not all that important, or even insurmountable. There is a common ground of thought. Take for example Hillary Clinton's project for health care reform. She found inspiration in European systems. And the debates raging in the US around this common ground of thinking, of markers, are responsible for influencing French intellectual life, although sometimes the impact takes years. Thus the social democratic ideology which laid the foundations for European left wings and politics, has been revised by John Rawls. In France, it took 15 years for Rawls to be translated. But his way of thinking finally penetrated. What are our intellectuals doing? They spend six weeks in the United States, participating in think tanks or teaching in universities. They come back full of ideas and can go for a year on the energy they have stored up. I'm only exaggerating slightly. As for when the right comes back into power, it always extols the successes of the American right and its themes, like "law and order." We have a phenomenal capacity to import things from America, even our ideas. Moreover, the sequence of events is startling. The Bill Clinton era corresponds to a time when the left dominated Europe: 11 out of 15 countries in the European Union were governed by the left. Gore lost because of what might be considered the American left, like the followers of Ralph Nader. At the same time, the Italian left lost because of Bertinotti from the far left. Then came Jospin's turn to be a victim (among others) of the far left.

On the other hand, the relationship to the State is different, just like the other sides of community life. The State in France, and elsewhere in Europe, protects. In the United States, charitable institutions do that for the most part. The American dream is to become as wealthy as possible in order to then become a great philanthropist. In the eyes of the French, that's the strategy of the Ancien Regime.[30] Another fundamental difference: When a government comes to power and as soon as a Cabinet member has been named, he has only one idea in mind: to pass his own laws. A Cabinet member who does not defend his own laws, his own rules, is instantly considered useless. In the United States, the contract governs. At the same time in France, the use of contracts is developing, the role and importance of judges are growing, importance of law is not declining, but appears less appropriate day after day.

An example of this would be the law for the 35 hour work week, which in France represents the ultimate stage in transforming society through laws. It has been imposed uniformly and royally and obviously does not mesh with the social reality. Another example would be the importance and role of civil service. They are from the same mold as French identity. And the French ambition today is to convince the entire European Union to adhere to a concept of life and economic and social rules that would include the presence of important, modern civil service. The counter-example of this would certainly be England after the cataclysm of Thatcherism, rather than the current American model. America seems more the stooge for a large part of public opinion.

You must admit that world news flew to the aid of the French conception, first with the black out in California, then with the one in New York. What did Bill Clinton's former secretary of Energy say? That although the American system had been completely privatized, it had obviously neglected the network's infrastructure: that's not a money-maker. And the Italian "black out" reinforced the European idea that society is better served when strong civil service exists in a country, especially in essential fields such as this, of course.

The criterion for the relationship to the State still remains decisive as ultimately, the dominant culture in France is egalitarian and egalitarianism comes from the State. The French remain more preoccupied with the sharing of resources under the auspices of the State, than with maintaining their level of creation.

Another example: Our relationship to immigration is not the same. Not that racism does not exist in the US, but immigration in its totality is conceived of as resourcing, like an eternal spring, because the United States represents the country of the second chance. A country like France is not a country for second chances. France is a country that has doubts about its meritocratic system and is criticized because it is considered to be reproducing that system, rather than overcoming it. For the dynamic of a country depends on desire and the organization of opportunities for the intellectual and social promotion of its citizens. France, like all countries in Europe, is closing its borders to immigrants, even though it needs them now and will need them even more in the future, given demographic decline. Reagan, in relation to current European politicians, comes out looking like a complete liberal with his great program of legislation favoring thousands and thousands of immigrants. Our relationship to identities and ethnic groups is totally different.

WELLS: I'll come back to the point, well, a couple of points: the history, one of pragmatism, one of rugged individualism. America is a land of opportunity, it's not a land of entitlement.

It's a land in which you can arrive with a nickel in your pocket, and emerge fabulously wealthy. It's also a land in which you can arrive with a nickel in your pocket and still have a nickel in your pocket at the end of your life. It depends on your initiative, your talent and depends very often on a great deal of luck. You made the point about France. I was very struck early in my life in France. We bought a house in Provence and we were having some work done and we were getting to know the young mason who was working for us and he was talking about the things he was really, really passionate about and what he really wanted to be was a *paysan*. And he said, "I would have been a *paysan*, I would have had my fruit trees and my vegetables, but my father was a mason, so I had to be a mason." And it was a concept that was so totally foreign to me, that he felt constrained by who he was and what his father had done, that it limited his chances, limited his possibilities. Even though it is probably harder and requires more skill to be a mason than to be a farmer. I remember hearing one of the ambassadors, it may have been Rohatyn in fact, talking about the very basic difference, a key to understanding the basic difference between French society and American society. For Americans, liberty is primordial. Liberty is what matters more than anything else. Again, it is the individual liberty to go have a second chance, to go start over. And in France, he said, it's very much the concept of *egalité*. It doesn't matter how much wealth there is, as long as at the end, everybody comes up more or less equal, so that there aren't vast divergences. We are a lot more tolerant. We in America accept differences and well-being far more easily. Just look at the latest tax-cut as an indication of how we accept that—a tax-cut that only favors the rich. It doesn't favor the poor people at all. It doesn't even favor the middle-class. It favors people who are enormously wealthy. But that's what America is. And that is one of its forces of strength. I think that America in recent years has neglected one of the key points of its Constitution which is to promote the general welfare: obligation of the government, obligation of this coming together, this convention, to promote the general welfare. It's taken care of a lot of other things, but it hasn't taken care of that. Of course the right in America would argue we do too promote the general welfare because we make it possible through a strong economy for people to move ahead, to achieve, to own a home, to be self-employed. We make it possible for them to raise their families, to retire in comfort, in security. But nevertheless, there's no assurance that that's going to happen. Again, it's a land of opportunity, it's not a land of entitlement. Let me see, you talked about social obligation, the social safety net. The current situation in America, again, it's fairly recent, you know there was the time of the great depression and Franklin Roosevelt. There was a great movement towards a far more socialized system. Much, much more support for everyone. Almost every social law was written in those times. Basically that was a political model that was maintained until Ronald Reagan. Even as recently as '64, the political campaign between Goldwater, a Republican of the right. He seemed far-right at the time, but was really fairly moderate. And Lyndon Johnson who was very much in the mold of Franklin Roosevelt. Lyndon Johnson pushed through laws ensuring a so-called Great Society, the Voting Rights Act which enfranchised blacks, basically, other more specific pieces of legislation that reinforced this thing. But what Americans feel they have found in attempting this is that it's an approach that has not worked as well as the market works. It has not worked as well, it creates big bureaucracy, therefore jobs at the Federal level. That would be popular in France, where one person out of four is a *fonctionnaire*. In America, that's not the perception. Again it comes back, I think, to being a caricature, to being overly simplistic. It comes back to the idea of the individual responsibility and individual rights and possibilities.

COLOMBANI: The aspirations of the European peoples in terms of philosophical and religious values, of sharing and social protection, relationship to authority, family structure—are similar from one European nation to another. And they are different from aspirations in America. We gave a quick overview. We could add to that the difference in how we approach diversity. France not only favors homogenization, it favors a certain idea of national community which is refractory to the idea of communities. Communitarianism is perceived more as a threat, a danger, whereas Americans give it space. There are no positive discriminations in France; only vague attempts to discuss the subject and one course offered in higher education at the Institut d'Etudes Politiques de Paris (The Institute for Political Studies in Paris). These policies familiar to the world of American Democrats, are always perceived, or denounced as contrary to integration. That goes back to the history of France, which has always been assimilationist. Moreover, French colonial policy was officially assimilationist. As if patriotism could be decreed. The United States is both much more patriotic and accepting of greater diversity. That is, more importance is placed on the community; discrimination is accepted. Even when it is negative, as in discrimination against poorer people or the most recent wave of immigrants; or positive, when aimed at correcting these excesses. French culture is still so totally refractory to the system, that French intellectual debate today focuses solely on the idea of the defense of the Republic through assimilation, which in turn is associated with standardization. Anyone disagreeing by defending a particular community would virtually be attacking the nation. There is a state of tension around what used to be the Jacobin model, in relation to what could have been a Girondin model or a decentralized France, taking its source of inspiration in de Tocqueville and perhaps even American democracy. But unfortunately, its enemies are communities! Hence the United States is the enemy, because it is the model for communitarian society, whereas France defends an integrationist model.

Personally, I do not share this stiff vision because for one thing, it's distorted and for another, the Jacobin model in France has become an obstacle to adaptation and modernization rather than the instrument of progress, that it had been in the past. Besides which, in order to make room for communities, the US had to be strongly united. No one is more patriotic than an American. This is witnessed by the importance of the American flag and the unique patriotic fervor it inspires. In comparison, the celebration of Bastille Day is more like a folk-holiday than a day of patriotic observance. Between France and America, there is almost a frontal shock in the way the debate is organized. And another good reason to denounce the American model is precisely that it is supposed to bring about destruction of the French State as well as the concept of the Republic as we idealize it today.

The French debate is, in fact, constantly imprinted with nostalgia. In dominating media circles, greatly influenced by "National Republican" thought—which to my mind, is purely and simply nostalgia and aspiration for nationalistic renewal, we are reconstructing and invoking the French model. With this difficulty however: When was the golden age of France? From 1802 to 1815? 1848 to 1870?[31] 1918 to 1940? Whenever. But it is clear that our intellectuals are against American communitarianism. We are in the very heart of a strong dissociation that has hit the elite and especially those at the executive level and the media. The executive level naturally tends to favor the model it serves, which is the Jacobin model. Here we are back at the beginnings of our two republics. And there, are two generals, Bonaparte and Washington: but one will become emperor, the other will give up his power. That is the overwhelming difference, of all our differences. Perhaps we are still feeling the consequences of that dissociation.

This is all the more anxiety provoking for us, as it seems that the French integrationist system is out of order. The greatest problem for the French is the suburbs, with which we are not, or hardly, dealing. Perhaps in the US this takes care of itself, with the first generation immigrants being necessarily lower class, while the second generation has the right to move to a higher level of wealth and so on. In France, we have difficulty accepting this positioning on different levels. And we have allowed the suburbs to amass a mountain of difficulties and have put young people, most of who are first-generation immigrants and the worst off, on the front line.

This is perhaps the heart of our differences. The United States knew how to come back to full employment. They got through the crisis years better than we did and the Clinton era was one of the most brilliant on an economic level. For us, since the two oil crises—that is for the past thirty years—massive unemployment has become the norm. And French society opted for massive unemployment in the negotiations held here. Between less interesting, lower paid jobs or agreeing to make sacrifices by reducing numbers of employees, they chose reducing numbers, leaving the State to deal with the unemployed. I even lived through it. In 1994, *Le Monde* was bankrupt. We had to implement a series of rigorous methods. I went to the unions to propose two solutions: lowering salaries or laying people off? The answer was instantaneous: lay people off. In other words, you dump responsibility for the people who leave on the community.

The French refuse to let anyone touch their famous acquired rights, a notion which is absolutely antinomic to life in the US. At the same time, when we adjust numbers, we take a thousand precautions. In the US, you tell someone to leave and if they are given two or three days to pack their things, they may be grateful. The French choice of massive unemployment was and still is profoundly devastating. Devastating because it keeps an entire population of young people on the sidelines: their parents have never worked, barely gone to school, lack the strict minimum for civic integration, to live in society. Society is living with this mass of people who have not integrated, who have not gone to school, with the temptation, as the philosopher says, to "watch over and punish." Obviously, this situation breeds violence. By refusing communitarianism, we leave communities to their fate. It becomes a sort of negative communitarianism. Is this reasonable? Therein lies a cultural, intellectual, ideological shock which is almost head-on and which is not to France's advantage.

WELLS: I think that's true. It's really that the solution that was chosen was really anti-French, because it created almost a permanent underclass of people who are disadvantaged, who will never be integrated into French society. You know, I know this is a problem. I know that there's a colossal difference, but I've never encountered this in all the things I've read or heard. I've never heard anybody say that a fundamental difference between the two countries, between the two societies was this. This cultural difference. It's real, but I don't think it's particularly a source of dispute. It's something that yes, is pointed to, if Americans are talking about the difficulty of doing business in France, of the things that they don't understand about France, yes, it's always pointed to, but I don't think it really, particularly plays in the current divisions between the two countries. I think that just one footnote on that situation, is that any time that Alcatel or Michelin lays off thousands of employees, they're always in the United States, they're never in Clermont-Ferrand.

COLOMBANI: It would start a revolution.

WELLS: It did! It did!

WELLS: I was very much taken with your statement that the French couldn't believe that Bush would go to war claiming to hear the voice of God, because it reminds me of Joan of Arc, or Bernadette. Many Americans talk to God and think that God talks to them. Again, it's something that distinguishes us, something that keeps us sort of puzzling over one another. There's a very strong tradition of Evangelism, of Christian-Protestant Evangelism in America. It's really one of the bases, the foundation of the country. It exists today and as it is currently, there have been periodic intense expressions of Christianity. These movements of rebirth, reborn Christianity. Once again, how do you explain beyond that? It's actually very simple. Just as the religion itself is very simple. It's just there. Again, an American expression: It's part of the wallpaper. It's not surprising that Bush, who's a man of some simplicity himself, would be intensely religious. There's also the factor, which is significant, that religion is very important in politics. It would be sort of unthinkable for a professed atheist to be elected president. We've elected a Catholic president. It's possible that we would elect a Jew as president. Certainly Lieberman, who is an Orthodox Jew, ran a very strong campaign. I think what's important in the electorate's mind is that religion play a part in a candidate's life. It doesn't matter so much what religion it is, although certainly a Muslim would have a lot of trouble getting elected in America. Elected to anything. So there are these two strains: there's the history and the importance in politics, and that's really what's playing in Bush's mind. You know, America is very deeply "churched," in a manner of speaking. Church is very, very important there. Churches are growing. Their power is growing. And they largely are churches that are on the religious right. Fundamentalist in their point of view. There's a "feel good" aspect to American Protestantism. You go to church to feel better. And you practice your faith in order to feel better. You feel better about yourself. You feel better about your fellow man, you feel better about your world. It's basic. It's important. That it would play such an important role in policy is surprising and it's very troubling. I think the increasing strength of the religious right is something to really worry about, because people who go to war to carry out the will of God are always a source of trouble. In Europe, you lived through your wars of religion. You are a good deal more suspicious of the effects of religion. You have perhaps come through this and perhaps you were never in it as intensely as America is, but it's something that is very problematic and of course it plays out not just in going to war against Iraq, but it also plays out in policy for Israel. It's one of the reasons that it's become almost impossible for the United States to play a meaningful role in solving the problems in the Middle East, because the religious right, though Christian, is totally committed to the Jewish state and against the pagans. What else is there to say? I would like to come back to the point though that hearing the voice of God is not uniquely American.

COLOMBANI: Opinion changes in Europe at the very moment that Bush talks about the "axis of evil," which has obvious religious overtones. In the beginning we had difficulty understanding why Bush developed a line of thought rigorously opposing the themes used by the terrorists to justify their combat. It is at precisely that moment that three European leaders speak up, in almost the same terms, to respond to this discourse. Chris Patten, European Commissioner, says things firmly. Joschka Fischer finds the best formula in saying, "We want to be partners and allies, we are not satellites." Hubert Vedrine, goes furthest in his analysis, speaking of the "simplism" of Bush's speech. And to come back to what we were saying, it is interesting to note that neither Chris Patten, nor Joschka Fischer are objects of the wrath of Washington; however, Hubert Vedrine is berated and the French Ambassador to Washington called in. But this brings us back to the same point about American behavior, where the president is headmaster and Europeans are the students. Whenever there's noise in the class, without even turning around the professor designates the French student as the author of the disturbance. Three European personalities use the same words to express their disagreement at the same time, but only the French Ambassador to Washington is called in to be pilloried.

This discourse on the "axis of evil" has religious connotations. It takes for granted that America is waging war in the name of Good. Faced with events aimed at "killing Jews or crusaders," the president goes on his own crusade. For us, this is the sign of regression. Why? Because we did not experience September 11th the same way. For us, this should have been when the US discovered its vulnerability. As we all do. For Europeans who have lived under threat for half a century from the Red Army, who have sustained and still suffer from daily terrorism in certain regions, it is important to encourage an Islam that aspires to dialogue, so that Islam turns away from Fundamentalism. Even if the tragedy in New York cannot be compared to waves of terrorism in Europe (in Paris, in particular), we feel that America should make an effort to no longer be "a city on a hill," as the Puritan Bible says, but rather a country like all others, that lives in the present, and hence is mortal. A country that, like all others, needs other nations and needs to invent new alliances, in order to consolidate those that already exist...anything but the unilateralist messianism that Bush extolled in his famous speech.

This regression is linked to religiousness. At any rate, as seen by an old secular country like ours. But at the same time, our secularism evolved. In the beginning, it was a weapon against Catholicism, against the historical tie between State and Church. The King of France was the incarnation of God on Earth. In Versailles, the king's bed was built like a tabernacle—it is a tabernacle and the body of God is the body of the king. In a country where the Church was so consubstantially linked with power, and absolute power at that, its secular laws constitute the successful emancipation of society with regards to the Catholic Church. Today, secularism is something else again. It's what allows everyone to follow his religion independently from government.

Government protects freedom of faith. With the return of religion, France must learn to live with an Islam that has become the second religion in the country. In the light of this religious phenomenon, secularism is put forward as a factor of integration, in a republican entity. What role does religion play in public life? Chirac attends mass when he is on vacation; he never misses the opportunity to send a message to the practicing Christian fringe of his electorate. But at the same time, Minister of the Interior Sarkozy, who is also minister of cults, appears at a meeting of the ultra-radical Muslim organization to say they must not wear the veil. That today, sends a much stronger and much more important message to the French than Chirac attending mass. Religion is definitely in the public eye, because of Islam and the fears it inspires, but not as a given of political life as it is in the United States. One doesn't elect someone because of his religion. The reference remains above all, secularism. Thus there is not only misunderstanding, but also profound rejection of the idea that one may wage war in the name of the Good one possesses against evil. That brings us back to the Huntingtonian[32] vision of the modern world, the West against the Muslim world. For us, this view is dramatically false and dramatically dangerous.

WELLS: Well, I think that the vast majority of Americans would agree that it's dangerous and that it's false. It's interesting that our constitutions are almost parallel in the way that they prohibit the establishment of religion. And yet, they protect religion. They protect any religious practice. America's going through a debate currently about two words: "under God." In our Pledge of Allegiance we say, "One Nation," and in about

1954 or something, it became "One Nation under God." There was objection to that of course and it's really questionable that it's constitutional and then it would probably be banned and then there will probably be a fight to have a constitutional amendment that would allow the practice of religion in state settings, whether it was schools or some government venue. Words are problematic. As I like to say, words have consequences that you don't always expect when you say them. Going back to the cases that you cite of Chris Patten and Joschka Fischer and Hubert Vedrine, the responses of Patten and Fischer were a good deal more modulated than that of Vedrine. To call a president of the United States "simple" is provocative. And Vedrine is an intelligent enough man to know that it would have that effect. It was not simply that the teacher without turning away from the blackboard said, "Ok, it's the French guy who did it." It came from a pattern, if only from Vedrine's constant reference to the United States as a hegemon, which is a word that really sets off Americans. They find that word pejorative. So maybe Bush felt justified in pointing his finger at Vedrine.

COLOMBANI: It wasn't the president who was under attack, only his words which were "simplistic." At the same time, it is true that Vedrine distinguished himself by coining the word "superpower," a term destined above all to alert opinion against the United States. Oddly enough, I feel that Vedrine is closer to Chirac than to Mitterrand. The former works in an anti-American framework, whereas the latter was always in an Atlantic frame of mind, whether by supporting Margaret Thatcher in the Falklands War or especially by supporting George Bush Senior in the Gulf War. Vedrine is undoubtedly unaware of the history of the democratic left: anti-Americanism has always been a weapon of the right to discredit the reformist left in France.

But to get back to the religious factor, there is a true split between the two sides of the Atlantic. As America is the country of sects. Bush is presented as a "born-again Christian." Here in France, that means he belongs to a religious category that is close to a sect. Added to that is the pressure from Christian fundamentalist groups applied to Bush's entourage, who claim responsibility for pushing Bush to side with the Israeli right. Christian fundamentalists, traditionally anti-Semitic, have become Islamophobic and now have moved over to the Israeli right. All of this has forged a disastrous image of Bush in the French media. George Bush is presented as spokesman for a current of Christian Fundamentalist thought, hence naturally a bearer of themes or reactionary ideas and of a reactionary foreign policy both linked to the hard core of the Israeli right and to the hard core of the military-industrialist establishment.

Whereas in France, there is a parliamentary commission, and condemnation of sects. The sect most often in the public eye is the Church of Scientology, which is regularly and heavily fined. One cannot speak of French resentment of the United States without mentioning Bush, and when mentioning Bush, without talking about this aspect, which may be exaggerated or abusive. The influence of Christian fundamentalists may be overestimated, but at the same time, it is perceived as major. It goes even so far as to erase the friendly overtures Bush made to the Muslim community, by showing a president wielding a minority philosophy to be sure, but very actively drawing America towards a sort of Christian radicalism, a new form of political action.

WELLS: I just approved a Scientology ad campaign for the paper, because of freedom of speech. It's not the revenue, because I turn down ads that are in bad taste, but for us it's a different set of values; freedom of speech is more important. And of course we have in America a tradition of religious tolerance. It's not particularly clear in all instances. It's interesting though that the religious right, the fundamentalism in the United States, is probably now the dominant religion, is probably the dominant expression of religion, whether it's through the Southern Baptist Convention, or very conservative branches of other denominations, cults or even through the Church of England. They are in essence—my brother's priest in one of them—in essence, they parallel the Lefebvre movement in France of some years back, or in Switzerland: the breakaway sect of the Catholic Church. And of course, movements like Opus Dei are much more developed here than they are in the United States because Catholicism is more widespread. I could not agree with you more that resorting to religion to defend policy, our politics, is extremely troubling. But it finds an audience in America. And I have no doubt that with Bush, it's very, very, very deeply felt. After Clinton's problems with Monica Lewinsky, and with the Congress, he turned to God in a sense. He had been raised as a Protestant, in the South, but he was associated more from that point on with Billy Graham and other semi-official men of the cloth. It's very much a factor in American life, certainly a factor in American political life. And by and large, it is a source of personal strength for these people. It's only when it becomes expressed in these extremely fundamental ways, that it becomes problematic. Is that again limited just to Bush? The only evidence we have so far is that it is. The only evidence that exists to this point is that it's characteristic of this administration and no other. It's very unlikely that a Democrat would ever be elected with the help of the religious right. And the religious right remains very much in a minority position. Most of America goes to church at Christmas and at Easter. Most of America is not particularly more churched than the French. Most of America spends Sunday watching TV or playing golf and not going to church. But the part that carries, the part that weighs heaviest is, you know, this intense commitment to Jesus.

COLOMBANI: Just let me say that the Monica Lewinsky affair would not have been to the credit of Bill Clinton, but it would not have hurt his chances for re-election. On the contrary, I think that it would have been perceived as... something reassuring.

WELLS: Not that that's the point of the discussion, but it was just an opportunity to get him. It was intensely political. They got him because he lied. He only lied about sex, he didn't lie about going to war.

COLOMBANI: I would say that the interests are even more relat-ed. Of course, there are commercial rivalries, but there we move away from the French-American relation, towards a relationship that might be Euro-American. There is both rivalry and partnership. But if one had to evaluate the situation, common interests win. These are two entities that structure the world economy. The rise in power tomorrow of China, India, Latin America and perhaps Africa someday, should bring these two entities closer together.

The interests are closely linked. Industry and European services are very largely financed by American pension funds. On the other hand, European participation in American industry is extremely frequent. There is an extremely close interweaving which causes both markets to move at the same time, or with just a slight time-lag. Even if particularities exist which allow America to advance more quickly. Even if Europeans today are slowly becoming aware that America has been able to reaccelerate in the past ten years, leaving Europe a little behind. This is seen in the growth rate, on a research level, and on the level of technology's performances. Europe is running late, and they are going to have to move from awareness to action to make up time. But we are all in a sphere where common interests go hand in hand with rivalries.

WELLS: Once again, we're in agreement. The two anecdotes that I think bear on this issue: In the state of South Carolina at the time of the disagreement, I was with one of the state legislators, an Assemblyman who introduced a resolution condemning France and it was quickly withdrawn when he realized that one of the state's largest employers is Michelin, which has a very big factory in Spartanburg. The second anecdote is that I think it was yesterday—it was this week anyway—that a member of Congress whose name I don't know, introduced, or was about to introduce, legislation that would forbid American armed forces from buying any French product. And the Defense Department reacted—rapidly and powerfully—to say this is ridiculous. We absolutely can't endorse this. We can't operate our armed forces if we are not buying telecommunications equipment. I believe that's the principal thing that the Pentagon buys from who—Alcatel? Thomson? Our interests are closely allied and will remain allied. The rivalry, if that's the right word, I think, is neither economic, political or cultural. It seems to me that it just comes down to emotionalism. And I think that that is stronger on the American side than on the French side. It's simply an emotional reaction to something—suddenly America is not dominating, America can't control. It's almost like a spat between spouses. It's like a spat between husband and wife. It seems to me it's more emotional than anything else. It certainly has been emotional in the current climate. It's certainly the odious noise that comes from Fox broadcasting and Fox newspapers and Murdoch newspapers. It's certainly emotionalism, it's not based on anything the least bit sensible. It truly is the response of simpletons.

3
The Transatlantic Partnership in Crisis

In 2002, the French intellectual Regis Debray, drew up a constitution of the United States of the West: the fusion of Europe and the United States under common leadership to counter-balance Islamic pan-Arabism and a rapidly developing China.[33] This type of plan implies the integration of Western Europe and the United States, including the abandon of the European states' foreign sovereignty. While it is undeniable that all liberal Western societies share a common destiny, recent heated exchanges among American and European allies prove that management of relations with the United States is dividing Europeans.

Today, many question the possibility of maintaining a Western geopolitical entity uniting an America determined to use its strength without restraint, and Europe, while certainly divided on many levels, still a fervent promoter of international law. Thus does Francis Fukuyama observe the "cracks in the western world," underlining that the "European position seeks to institute an international order based on rules adapted to the post–Cold War world. Free from sharp ideological conflicts and large-scale military competition, this world makes much more room for consensus, dialogue and negotiation in the way it solves its problem....

The disagreement is not about the foundations of liberal democracy, but almost on the limits of democratic legitimacy. Americans are inclined to believe that there is no democratic legitimacy beyond the constitutional, democratic Nation-state.... On the contrary, Europeans tend to believe that democratic legitimacy stems from the will of an international community much larger than any Nation-state, no matter whom, acting by itself."[34]

While the use of force is a particularly vivid stumbling block, the debate is more generalized. In fact, here are two visions of the contemporary world at arms. Both bring into play very different perceptions of the new problems of security and the threat of terrorism; of multilateral action and international organizations; of the domination of the American empire or of an eventual multi-polar structuring of the world, of the Atlantic Alliance and the role of Europe within the Alliance. All in all, the transatlantic partnership seems deep in crisis.

WELLS: Americans are known for their impatience and particularly for impatience with things that don't work. The process leading up to the crisis over Iraq revealed two things that, for the Bush administration, didn't work: the UN, and the Atlantic partnership. Regarding the first, there is a long and troubled relationship between the UN and the growing body of American conservatives. Those resolutions over the years condemning Israel and equating Zionism with racism haven't endeared the institution to anyone who is committed to Israel's right to exist. And the absurdity of giving Libya the chairmanship of the UN's Human Rights Commission doesn't even merit comment or examination. That it happened with the acquiescence of France (and six other members of the EU, who also abstained in the vote) is an embarrassment and an outrage. Why, Libya is not yet free from United Nations penalties that were imposed because of the Lockerbie bombing. That is just one example of how the

UN and its institutions have been abused and degraded and lost their relevance as tools for world peace.

As the UN has been turned into a vehicle where dictatorships like Iran and Libya can try to embarrass the United States, while Europeans stand by, who can blame Americans for losing patience with this "talk shop" as well as with those who see it as the only forum for action on the world stage. Not just atavists like Jesse Helms,[35] and not just the pro-Israel neo-conservatives, but a large number of Americans have lost patience. Most of Bush's counselors opposed going back to the UN with the Iraq issue because the UN had only wobbled and waffled for the past decade and avoided "humiliating" a genocidal killer.

Now, in the context of the Atlantic partnership, the trouble over Iraq didn't start with the UN, it started with NATO, when France tried to use NATO against the intentions of the Bush administration. When the Atlantic partnership turned into another theater for trying to break the will of the Bush administration, it set the stage for a damaging confrontation between the arrogance of American power, and another kind of arrogance— of French powerlessness.

There was an interesting construct by an old colleague of mine in the days before the Iraq showdown, the late Flora Lewis, who said that the US doesn't want to run the world, but it wants to be acknowledged as the nation most able to run it. From another perspective, when the United States defines Public Enemy No. 1, it wants everyone else to accept the definition and to put up the wanted posters too. Or at least not tear down the posters it has put up.

By attempting to block NATO aid to Turkey in the event of war with Iraq, I wonder if Chirac thought that would be an effective diplomatic approach. Surely he wasn't attempting a power play, because there was a clear path around his attempt at interposition. Whatever his motives, I can tell you how it played in the United States. It played as typical French bloody-mindedness.

Not France the great force for international morality, but of France ever the contrarian.

On the question of multilateralism, there is, in the way this question has been framed, an assumption that America has rejected a multilateral approach to foreign policy because it rejected French interposition on Iraq. And I dispute that. First of all, it's worth pointing out that multilateralism is not a goal in itself, but a means to a goal. As a means unto itself, it turns into talk shop multilateralism, flaccid and pointless. Secondly, historically the US has always rejected attempts to impose limits when it sees a need for action to protect its interests and its citizens. That is implicit in the Monroe Doctrine, and it has been evident numerous times in our history. (As an aside, let me say too that the British and the French practiced multilateralism with Hitler in 1936. If they had stood up to him, the world would be a different place today.) Finally, you can't say that just because France didn't support the action to remove Saddam Hussein from power—or France and Germany and Russia and another score of countries—the march on Baghdad was a unilateral act by the US. Bush had the support of the British, the Australians, the Dutch, the Japanese, the Poles and Czechs. More than 30 countries in all were on-the-record supporters of the US-led effort, and there were private endorsements from another score. Some of those who signed on had more to fear from France than from the United States, as Chirac sought to make clear to the Poles and others. One account I read[36] said there were 45 official and unofficial members of the coalition, which would make it the third largest ever. There were 47 partners in World War II action, and 51 in the Bush I coalition to chase Iraq out of Kuwait.

So whether you defend the removal of Saddam as something that had to be done, or detest Bush for going to war illegally, I don't think you can say it was a unilateral action carried out without regard for the opinion of mankind.

Perhaps from the perspective of the spurned, the US under Bush is increasingly a dangerous Lone Ranger, riding off on unbridled, capricious missions, without regard for what any other country wants or thinks. But the evidence shows otherwise. The negotiations over North Korea are clear evidence of a multilateral approach to a very huge problem. The US has also expanded NATO and worked within it. It has strengthened the OSCE,[37] created NAFTA, APEC[38] and the WTO. And it has integrated new partners (and former adversaries) into these organizations. None of that represents the approach of an arrogant Lone Ranger or a rogue state charting its own course without regard or respect for others.

COLOMBANI: This brings to mind a distinction initiated by the American intellectual Joseph Nye,[39] in *The New York Review of Books*, from an analysis which corresponds well to our way of thinking. According to his thesis, the mistake Bush makes is to mix up all levels: military, economic, cultural and civil. No one can deny that the United States enjoys unequalled, unheard-of military supremacy. In a sense, this military supremacy is to our advantage, we Europeans, as it allows us to forgo an enormous defense effort that would weaken us economically. In fact, Americans are capable of being on several fronts, leading several conflicts in different parts of the globe at the same time. From this point of view, the American setbacks in Iraq give the impression of a colossus with feet of clay being tripped up by anti-A m e r i c a n vulgate. Whether we like it or not, this is bad news for Europe.

Let's get back to superpower. The mistake is to transpose this superpower to other levels of collective life. On an economic level, the United States is no longer a superpower. To be sure, they are leaders. Currently they are a driving force— Europe certainly keeps its eyes riveted on the American indexes in order to set its own economic rhythms. But the US is not hegemonic. The European economy exists. The Chinese economy is taking off. The Japanese economy, while weak now, was one of the driving forces of world growth. The Indian economy is looming up and will be one of the determining factors in future years. Russia has committed to reconstruction, even if it takes ten to fifteen years. The Latin American zone is beginning to take shape. One has only to observe the debates taking place at the WTO, to understand to what extent it is false to imagine that the US can impose its commercial will on China, India, Europe. In all these fields I would say the United States participates, like everyone does. In economic matters, multilateralism prevails. The mistake Bush Jr. makes is to believe that superpower combined with economic hegemony also induces superpower on a third level, in societal life. He forgets that globalization, especially since the fall of the Berlin wall, was before and still is, a democratic globalization. Since 1989 democracy has progressed. And civil populations have their own life. Public opinion exists: in Europe, Arab states, Latin American countries, Canada, Asia, etc.... and none of them wants to take orders from the White House, run by Reverend George Bush. That doesn't impress anyone. Moreover, our opinions are more concerned by what are now called non-governmental organizations (NGOs), the increasingly important role they play in communities, and their tendency towards omnipresence. From now on, to believe one might rule the world through military superpower, imposing hegemony on all aspects of collective life, citing examples of this ranging from the war in Iraq to Hollywood life, is to show great imagination. At least, that seems to me to be the dominating point of view in Europe today, and the most pertinent.

Paradoxically, unilateralism is the modern form of isolationism. Contrary to appearances, as unilateralism is bringing the US to foreign fronts, it is all the more isolationist, since on an economic level, it is accompanied by protectionism.

WELLS: You are perceptive in your analysis of unilateralism as isolationism, because that it surely is—the Rogue Ranger. But as I said earlier, even with the intensity of the debate over Iraq, (and a debate, I might add, that grows more emotional as the war grinds on and its costs to the American economy become known), I don't think America is moving into a period of rogue unilateralism. Isolationism has several faces, and in fact, the variety that's most frightful in today's world is that of the modest and earnest—those who would like to see America as no more than an equal, those who don't think that superpower status engages responsibilities. A Jimmy Carter isolationist, in other words. The truth is that America cannot afford isolationism in an age in which not just trade is globalized, but terrorism is too.

I don't think we see America as a rogue state led by savages. What we do see perhaps is a superpower struggling to relate to this new world, where the enemy uses all of the benefits of a free and open society as tools to destroy that society. The United States is struggling because of the scope and nature of the threat that the West and the US in particular now face. A struggle like the current one leads to errors—errors in judgment, errors in diplomacy. Errors, for example, like repressing human rights through excessive searches and arrests, and illegal incarceration. But that doesn't mean that we should forgo the struggle.

As we face this threat in my country, there's a very strong feeling that what's good for America is good for the civilized world, and we're able to define what's good for America—we don't need any help in figuring it out. So the challenge is to arrive at national protection through intense, highly developed multilateral cooperation.

So far, I'd have to say that the American administration is running a serious risk of losing sight of the pre-eminent goal, which is dealing effectively with terrorism. It substituted an immediate goal of toppling Saddam without adequate explanation of how that fit into the overall picture, and even more problematic for his strategy, without preparing adequately for the war and its aftermath. We seem to have toppled Saddam, and created a climate for hundreds of new Osamas. We may not have the Lone Ranger, but it does appear that there are some cowboys riding that range.

All that being said, I do not dispute for a nanosecond the need to take every precaution possible to avert another 9/11.

COLOMBANI: But that rule also applies to the French side. When we observe French leaders—Chirac or Villepin, it is astounding to see how obsessed they are with the United States. Everything is brought to an American level. As a result, if we believe them, any action we undertake should be the opposite of what America does. It's as if the point is not to build with them, and even less to influence their way of thinking or acting, but, more brutally, to mark points against them. All this, to take advantage of public opinion, especially in the Arab world, which is hostile to America.

I am suspicious of this attitude, because of history. We remember that in 1962, de Gaulle supported the U.S when their vital interests were threatened. Four years later, he left NATO with a bang and American bases in France were closed. France had the plague. From the French point of view, that was without doubt more traumatic than what we are experiencing today, especially for the French regions where the American bases were implanted, as they were a source of prosperity. This was a blow from the outside as well as the inside. The US perceived that as a betrayal, and all the more so as just before, France recognized Mao's Communist China. What happened in between? De Gaulle had unsuccessfully tried to draw the United States into the idea of a worldwide directorate. What did France want? To participate in it. The idea was not to constitute a coalition against American hegemony— American imperialism as they say, somewhat justified at the time. The purpose was to partake of the power. France moved away from the US at the time, because they refused to share their power. One may ask today, *mutatis mutandis*, if the underlying, unexpressed, unconfessed reproach of French leaders today with regards to American leaders, is to not have been more closely associated with the defining of strategy—of having been neglected, just as Great Britain neglected the rest of the world in the second half of the 19th century, because of its strength. Perhaps on the part of the French, there is disappointment at no longer being the privileged ally, as being recognized as the leader in Europe. But of course, this brings us back to the major characteristic of Europe today, which is the decline, if not the loss of Franco-German leadership. From Presidents Giscard d'Estaing and Mitterrand, Jacques Chirac inherited governance of the principality, or the co-principality, of Europe. In my eyes, he has partially squandered it: he is no longer recognized as co-Prince of Europe.

WELLS: It's interesting that you paint a picture of rejection and disappointment as explanation for the history of bad relations between our governments. Having his proposal turned down must have been personally bitter for de Gaulle, who had been rejected for such a long time by Roosevelt during the war, and embittering also of course because it was that *certaine idée de la France* that was being spurned. Perhaps Americans were motivated by what happened under the previous Directoire that France was noted for. But that history of rejection might very well have contributed to an obsession in the way that France—now in the persons of Chirac and Villepin—looks at the United States and a parallel obsession about controlling American power. One editorialist wrote at the height of the bad feelings between our two countries that it was more important to France to control American power than it was to control Saddam Hussein. An overstatement, no doubt, but one containing, like your theory of rejection, at least a hint of truth.

There's a second element of that obsession, though, and it recalls one of the facets of the Soviet Union's relationship with the United States throughout the Cold War. I mean an obsession about being taken seriously by the Americans and treated as important. Some of our diplomats who have worked on Franco-American relations have said that America thinks that France is constantly testing it, and putting roadblocks in the path. We think that France insists that America make special efforts to show the French that we're friends and take you seriously.

There's another current example of that: the settlement with Libya over the Lockerbie deaths. At the moment a settlement is reached, the French say "No, we're going to block it, because you didn't take care of us and our UTA DC-10." Again, it sure looked like bloody-mindedness.

But to come back to Iraq, the Canadians were opposed to the war too, and on moral grounds, like America's other partners in NAFTA, the Mexicans. But it's the Canadians who are the best example, because Canada is a country that is known for right-thinking, moral positions on international issues. You can't say we're not close—we share the longest unprotected border in the world. And you'd be wrong to say we've got them in our pocket, because they oppose us on a great many issues. As they did on Iraq. But they made their point and then kept quiet. France was not able to do that, was not able to take a moral position and have recourse in that. Instead, there France went lobbying for support of its position.

Did Chirac do that to enforce the moral position? Or did he do it as a power play, to demonstrate that France had to be reckoned with, and that the risk of showing disrespect for France would have serious consequences? Of course, Americans have two other explanations. I don't subscribe to them, nor do I practice the kind of cynicism that they represent. But on the other hand, I've never heard a refutation of either. The first is that Chirac's course of action wasn't moral at all, but a cynical sop to France's growing and sometimes militant Islamic population. His Algerian tour at the same time would have played to the same domestic audience.

The second is that since France had sold Iraq not just the Osiraq nuclear reactor, which Israel destroyed 20 years ago, but, according to records that Iraq made available to the UN, 21 percent of the "equipment" used for making chemical weapons. The hardcore cynics say France was fighting to keep a client. A slightly more generous explanation is that France didn't want the embarrassment of a wide disclosure of everything it was selling to the Iraqis.

I know very well that those are not questions that will ever have a public answer.

COLOMBANI: The first point seems indisputable to me. Moreover, Jacques Chirac can be proud of having defended a consensus position in internal affairs. If there had been a presidential election at the onset of the war in Iraq, he would have won by 102 percent! Concern over a strong Muslim minority, anxiety about the possible rise of violence in what we call the "hood"—that is, suburbs where there is a concentration of all the ills of French society, beginning with the disinheritance of the children of recent immigration—were all elements of the French position. On the other hand, I cannot accept your accusation of economic cynicism. Not that France is incapable of it. France uses and abuses just like everyone else, and cynicism might have pushed us to participate in the war in the hopes of profiting from the spoils of post-war contracts, along with Halliburton. No, I am afraid that the cynicism you speak of is that of the American Vice President.

I remember the Davos meeting, winter 2003. Everyone was focused on the perspective of war. Two American speakers were the stars: Attorney General Ashcroft, and Colin Powell, the diplomat. Ashcroft froze the audience with his brutal, closed vision. On the other hand, Powell developed the notion of the "benevolent empire." He explained that America was well into a process that led to war, the main purpose of which was to find weapons of mass destruction (today we know that they were more of a pretense than a reality). It was also immediately confirmed that America was not going to war for ideological reasons, nor to establish an empire, and even less to create a sort of protectorate in that region of the world. No, they were going to war to assume their role as a "benevolent" power. Powell recalled, in fact, that in history, the US left its borders to do the dirty work its allies asked it to do—i.e., restore order in the world, restore democracy where it had been beaten—and its mission having been accomplished, to go home. Hence, it would not go to Iraq to remain there after Saddam Hussein was eliminated. It would leave when democracy had been established and return to its main activity, i.e., its vocation of being a commercial republic, a market republic, the progress of which was due to exchange and not conquest. Along the same lines, if you look carefully at the American task force in Iraq, it seems to me that the American soldiers—except the Special Forces—are not behaving like judges or conquerors, but seem above all anxious to return home and get back to quiet, peaceful lives. We are far from Roman legions and even farther from the armies of the young French Republic going forth to establish other republics in Italy, under the orders of General Bonaparte. A priori, how could one not believe Colin Powell, who is also a "benevolent" personality? But he must well know, having learned it at West Point, that a democracy can not be an empire. We come back to the notion of multilateralism, the same notion that challenges the new American strategic doctrine.

What is the basic difference with the past? In the second half of the 20th century, because the US was the liberator of Europe and the most powerful nation, it organized a coalition under its command, the purpose of which was to contain the Soviet bloc. At the time of this doctrine an idea was imposed: that everything had the same starting point, Washington and the American national interest, and all the rest drew from that. Exactly like the expression you use, "what's good for America, is good for us," in fact. From that definition comes the mission of American national interest. Once this mission was defined by Washington, preferably by the Defense Department and not the State Department—which makes all the difference—a coalition had to be formed. This coalition constituted a variable geometry, according to the territory and purpose of the mission. This was hence a doctrine totally opposed to the one which bound Europe to the United States for fifty years: up until then, the cement between Europe and the United States was a coalition based on common defense. This coalition was based on the idea that our essential, vital interests are shared. Henceforth, we are no longer defining common concerns, but rather observing the national American interest, which assigns and describes its mission. And after that? Well, "If you love me, follow me!" The English will always follow of course, but the others, like us, are not necessarily obliged to follow a plan which by definition is nationalistic, and sovereign, as the Canadians would say. The heart of the problem resides in this change of strategic parameters. And not in the notion of benevolence. We know all too well that the US is not going to make Iraq the 51nd state.

Besides the fact that the notion of empire is contrary to the very idea that we want to export, i.e., democracy, it must be linked to this new strategic doctrine, which again, defines *stricto sensu* the American national interest from which coalitions are made. Here we are at the bottom of the ditch of transatlantic discord. To that, one must add a massive argument at the center of this new strategic doctrine, that makes any European who wishes to see a European identity emerge, tremble: Any American defense effort today, whether economic or technological, must be achieved in a way that no other state be allowed to "catch up" to the United States. We are no longer faced with a statement of a common strategic doctrine designed to tighten the Atlantic community, but with a declaration of economic, technological, political wars with allies of the United States, or at least with those allies who do not share this vision of the world. Those who do not follow are confronted with what might legitimately be considered a form of declaration of hostilities to come. It is a seignorial speech, like a lord to his vassals in the Middle Ages. What regression!

In France, Regis Debray, who is considered a great intellectual, inspired Hubert Vedrine, former Minister under François Mitterrand and Jacques Chirac, with the idea of the "United States of the West," to characterize the new American policy. Besides the fact that he is often wrong, I am always in total disagreement with Regis Debray, his vision of the world and especially his concept of the US. Except when we see this new American strategic doctrine unfold before our very eyes, how could one not realize that the US itself is feeding anti-Americanism to the ideological sharks? Because we are in the presence of an imperial doctrine. So what if the empire is synonymous with the word "benevolent"? We still are not interested in the empire. France had a first empire, then a second, "liberal" empire beginning in 1860. Their ends were tragic, both marked by military adventures. Empires always end tragically. Better to avoid them.

WELLS: Yes, empires usually finish badly, but agreeing with that statement is not an acknowledgement that America is an empire. Theodore Roosevelt was our most empire-minded president, but before going to war to chase Spain out of Cuba he had to promise not to make Cuba a colony. That's probably another foreign policy decision that a lot of Americans would have liked to undo at a number of points over the last 50 years. And at the Bay of Pigs perhaps we were about to try.

I know it's too literal, but it's hard for me to dissociate the notion of empire from the notion of territory. France has experience with empires, the US has very little. It is often said that in all the wars the US has fought—has been called to fight—it has never claimed more than the territory necessary to bury its dead. Emotionalism, but it has the virtue of being true. The notion of empire recalls the Napoleonic era, a period when the quest for empire spread complete disorder all over the Continent. And again today we face the kind of disorder that the threat of terrorism spreads.

Recalling a more recent empire, the Soviets, today's world can again be divided in two: not into an east and west, dominated by the Soviets and the Americans, but into a world of order, led by America, and a world of disorder, led by Kim Jong Il and Saddam Hussein and Osama bin Laden.

"Empire" is a word that we actually have a reflex against in America because our experience with empire is negative—being part of the British Empire, watching Napoleon wreak havoc in the name of empire, watching Hitler build a particularly brutal empire of enslavement, dealing still today with the consequence of the withdrawal of the British and the French from their 19th and 20th century imperial policies. Jefferson spoke of an "Empire of Liberty" as he made the Louisiana Purchase and pursued the westward expansion. That was before the more politically acceptable phrase "manifest destiny" became the acceptable description. I actually have not been able to find the words "benevolent empire" coming from Colin Powell's mouth—I spent some time looking for the reference, only because I thought it curious that an American secretary of state would have used the word "empire" to describe American policy. Officially we don't like even "hegemony," so I was skeptical that Powell himself had adopted the "benevolent empire" label for the policies he helps to construct. At Davos, Powell did talk about building trust among nations and about America's responsibility in the world. It's clear that in Iraq we failed to build sufficient trust.

But this is perhaps quibbling. It may not have been Robert

Kagan who coined the phrase, but he developed arguments about American benevolence—that means "doing good," remember, not "doing bad"—in a paper published in 1998.[40] Clinton was the president, and Kagan introduced his argument by describing the concerns he had read being expressed abroad, including in France, about the risk to the world when American was consumed by a silly domestic political issue. The concern wasn't superficial, but regarded as legitimate. Was this improbable American pre-occupation with the president's sex life going to cause the world's economic locomotive to lose its power? Would the several tinder-boxes—the Balkans, the Korean peninsula, the Middle East—get ignited while America was distracted?

It's interesting to go back and read Kagan's paper now if only for the context of the time. There was another context, too, though Kagan doesn't mention it. America was threatening then to intercede against Saddam Hussein unilaterally. Madeleine Albright said after a tour of the Middle East in 1998 to solicit support for action against Saddam Hussein: "We should prefer to act multilaterally, but if necessary we shall act unilaterally." Of course they didn't—Clinton got caught up in the Monica Lewinsky scandal, and rather than "wag the dog," he let the UN wobble on rather than confront Saddam. France, Russia and China led the accommodationists then, too.

But back to the Kagan's notion of America as a "benevolent empire"—though I would prefer the older term of America's "sphere of influence," one that usually now includes Russia, by the way, as well as most other countries of the East Bloc. Even if I have a semantic problem with the characterization, there's no quibble with America's status as the world's only superpower. And there's no argument from me either that some of the ways it has exercised power have been imperious, and that has stirred deep resentment. In his 1998 paper, Kagan offers the supposition that it's not hubris that drives America now into sometimes high-handed behavior, but weariness. The existence of the Soviet Union imposed a discipline on the West that's not there anymore. The new global enemy, terrorism, is not monolithic like the Soviet empire and is therefore incorrectly perceived as less dangerous for the world. And so there's less unity on the questions of how do we deal with it. We thought we should start with Afghanistan and Iraq. Others thought that there could be no solution as long as the Palestinian issue isn't resolved.

Whatever word is applied—empire, superpower, or maybe Madeleine Albright's phrase, "the indispensable nation"— America's position derives from two factors, from its military power and its economic power. And both of those sources of strength emerged from World War II. The system put in place after the war was so beneficial to the nations decimated by war ("beneficial" is a word much like "benevolent") that it became entrenched, to the point that it probably cannot be undone. It has made Europe rich—and it has resulted in soft power being the only kind that Europe has *vis-à-vis* the United States. So in that situation, what Kagan calls "honorary multipolarity" is the only kind that's open to Europeans, either independently or collectively. America can cede power to Europe, Europeans can be "appointed" an equal partner. But what sort of equality does that imply? None at all—in fact, it implies the contrary. It speaks of condescension and paternalism, and also speaks of an eventual un-appointment, of for instance "old Europe" being replaced by "new Europe" as honorary multipolarity partner.

Economic power is more problematic, as Jean-Marie has rightly pointed out. Not only does Europe's economic strength rival America's, but the devolution of economic strength to India, to China, to other countries in Asia, Latin America and eventually, surely, in Africa, too, has not happened without the loss of economic power in the United States. The manufacturing sector is of particular concern as factory jobs slowly disappear from the US and shift to areas where it's less expensive to operate. That does not include Western Europe, however. I think more European factories are moving to the United States than in the opposite direction. That must be as much of a concern for Europe as it is for America, where economists worry that this trend will turn us into neo-have-nots. American's won't be able to buy from overseas sources the things that used to be manufactured in the United States. Presumably at that point too America would no longer be able to afford the military might that has given it the weight it sometimes throws around.

And at that point, this thing that I resist calling the American empire would end badly, as empires usually do.

COLOMBANI: One of the consequences of America's unilateralism and new strategy is that Europe no longer enjoys the same leniency on the part of the United States. For fifty years the US considered Europe a necessary evil and whether or not the government in power at the time was more or less favorable, the idea still dominated that building up Europe was good for the West. Obviously so, as the reconstruction of Europe, in the beginning, was one of the prime elements of a free Europe in the face of the Soviet bloc. The hurdle at the end of the Cold War was difficult to get over. George Bush Senior handled it with intelligence, with regards to Germany, by not questioning the process of European unification. The Europeans exchanged acceptance of unification with the Germans—to tell the truth, could they do anything but accept it?—against the strong anchorage that Germany had in Europe through the euro. We owe this historic "deal" to Helmut Kohl and François Mitterrand and their capacity to make the "common European good" triumph. You must remember that at the time, Germany's currency seemed strong and that offering it up to the euro constituted a great sacrifice. However, we were living in a context where the US accepted and even encouraged the European Union.

Henceforth, the attitude is inverted. The idea that the US has become hostile to European unification has taken hold in France. And that they might even want to dismantle it, since it no longer corresponds to their interests. The US, with the help of Great Britain, will only accept Europe (and this has always been the case for British diplomacy) on the condition that it remain a mere free-trade zone and not a territory aimed at becoming a political power. However, the traditional concept of Europe, which reconciled France and Germany, is fundamentally based on one objective: the progressive edification of an identity and European strength. Things are happening now as if the US had rallied around the concept, dear to Conservative Brits, of a free-trade zone, a vast, unique, and open market—which it is already—and are maneuvering to undo and divide Europe. Hence the London-Madrid-Warsaw axis, that is designed to oppose the Paris-Berlin axis and impose a vision of Europe as weak and disorganized, where the US may draw on its supply of allies according to its needs, to accomplish one or another of its goals, according to the doctrine "the mission defines the coalition." Such a concept obviously is a frontal attack against the idea we have of the European destiny, or unification. Moreover, the weapon the US uses is NATO, which is no longer considered to be a mere military alliance, but has become a political weapon in a framework concurrent with the European Union, in which the former Eastern bloc countries are being incorporated and with whom we are forming a political alliance, much stronger than with Russia. The major change lies in the fact that the United States is perceived as an enemy of the building of an integrated European Union. And that changes the way we perceive the United States considerably.

WELLS: I know there is an assumption that the United States is intent on destroying the European Union. But I don't think there's any proof of that, except the kind that comes in on talk radio, meaning the kind of proof that callers to my newspaper, and perhaps yours, too, have of some vast conspiracy.

Leaving talk radio aside: Sometimes in the relations between nations, as in the relations between men, you have to take people at their word. What do we know about America's attitude toward Europe and its wishes for the EU? President Bush has said: "We welcome a Europe that is truly united, truly democratic and truly diverse—a collection of peoples and nations bound together in purpose and respect, and faithful to their own roots."[41] We have had disputes over things like bananas, but no serious, disruptive fights about objectives or methods since the founding of the Common Market after World War II.

As for NATO, we see it as a military alliance, not a political one. We see it as an alliance that involves us, as well as Canada, in meaningful and effective ways with Europe, for a common purpose.

The real question about the European Union is not whether it's under threat from America. Rather, just how much union can Europe achieve? There's more than there was certainly in 1939. There's more than there was in 1962. But the Union is still a collection of nations, nations that remain very reluctant to give up their sovereignty, very resistant to burying their identity in any common purpose except a common economic purpose. And even that purpose is being approached with—do I call it multipolarity?—because of weak economies in France and Germany, and the need to spend beyond what the group decided on, borrowing limited to 3 percent of the GDP.

I know that it was a lot easier to create a United States of America than to create a united Europe. Our forebears started with a wilderness and imposed a nation on it. And they imposed that nationality on the waves of immigrants who arrived, too. Europe has started with 6 then 12 or 15 and now 25 individual nations, each with a strong identity, each with a proud history, each with different allegiances, each with a different approach perhaps towards solving their problems. And that's the real challenge for Europe—achieving unity, not fending off threats from across the ocean.

If the president of the European Union doesn't realize the impact of his words when he calls somebody a Nazi, and then a German calls the Italians fools, you know, this is certainly just a footnote in the development of the European Union, but it's a good story for the summer anyway.

COLOMBANI: Well you had Spiro Agnew—we have Berlusconi.

WELLS: Well, we didn't let Agnew stay in office once his outrages were found out.

COLOMBANI: It's all a question of size: Depending on whether you are short or tall, you see the glass half-full or half-empty. When it comes to Europe, the Americans see it as almost empty. Like Henry Kissinger's famous line, "Europe? What's the phone number?" I think you have to admit that little by little the phone number is being distributed. Perhaps you must tell Americans that Europe is about to adopt a constitution. It's a modest Constitution, to be sure. And it will not change the major economic reality that the US has allotted meager resources to their community budget. It will not lead to federalism, but will lay the basis for a "federation of nation states." And in too many respects, it maintains majority rule that will give the English, Polish and French votes the right to veto; hence so many more possibilities to block legislation in the name of nationalism. It will still be the first step towards a political statement without precedent in history. Firstly because we are dealing with, as Walter said, old nations which throughout their histories have torn each other apart and annihilated each other. Because successively, Venice, Rome, Lisbon, Madrid, Berlin, London, Amsterdam, Paris, are cities, even countries, which one by one dominated the world. The fact that these nations came to the conclusion that their destinies were not solitary or imperial, but should be merged, is also, once again, without precedent in history. That the road is long is obvious. That Europe, since its adoption by twelve countries, and the adoption of the common euro currency, seems at the end of its rope, is obvious. But ever since the Treaty of Rome, Europe has constantly progressed in ten-year cycles. The latest cycle is the common currency. The next will be a constitution. Other stages will follow, perhaps even at different speeds, in the construction of this Europe, as its growth to twenty-five states has been poorly prepared. That will be the task of those in power, who are bound to the idea of a common destiny: to constitute a hard core that will prevent them from being whittled down into a mere free-trade zone, a plan which would please the United States more than a politically strong Europe. Meanwhile, there has been no civil war, no conquering of the West. It is true that the two previous world wars were inter-European civil wars writ large. Europeans have no lessons to give. Suffice it to say that they have learned their lessons from history and that these lessons have brought them together. And from that point of view, their march forward is as exemplary as it is obstinate and opinionated. While from the onset, it did not take opinions into account, now it is progressing with the support of these opinions. You can judge by the consensus all over France in favor of including former Eastern bloc countries. This was a considerable surprise for both parties: the members letting them in and the nations who were joining. I am among those who regret how slow in coming the political Constitution is, as well as how weak the economic Constitution is. But the "little" that has come out so far, has been a driving force. France did not truly reach a level of modern progress until it was anchored to Europe.

And that is also the case for the other countries that founded the European Union. Europe has been the main lever that has allowed nations to modernize and progress like they never had before in their economic history. Just look at the rhythm of Spain and Portugal yesterday and at Greece today, without mentioning the most impressive example, which is Ireland. There is no more cursed land that Ireland; a land of such poverty and destitution, that many Irish sought refuge in America; a colony that had been tortured by Great Britain for centuries, and where today the average wage is equal to that of England. What a victory! What brought that to Ireland? The European Union, don't you think? Thus one might say that it is only economic. But economic progress in itself is a considerable thing, because it has conquered an historic curse. Poverty in Franco's Spain resembles the poverty in some African nations today. Ask some of the Moroccan elite how they intend to bring their country out of poverty. By coming closer to the European Union. The European Union is a phenomenal political idea, an extraordinary idea, full of unexplored, unexploited potential. Let's be patient!

In this current phase of crisis with regards to the transatlantic relationship (the point of departure of a united Europe was in fact the Marshall Plan), one must be very careful about the American attitude. One cannot preserve or nourish a transatlantic community without having a confirmed, European pillar. Personally, the error which I feel the current French leaders have made is to consider that a European identity can only be forged by opposing the United States. From de Gaulle to Mitterrand, not forgetting Giscard D'Estaing, the attitude that Chirac has adopted towards George Bush has, for the moment, weakened the French position and especially its capacity to further French goals. It's easy to grasp: Since Atlantic rules no longer include the United States, France has decided to free itself from their influence. Okay. But riding on the crest of their wave, the Chirac-Villepin duo decided to go one step further by taking the lead of the opposition against American policy, which, one must admit, has a majority in the Old World. This attitude, which consists of opposing America whenever possible, has in fact helped Washington to divide Europe. On the contrary, I feel that the European Union must be built with the US. Let's hope that the US doesn't turn its back on the European Union. We await the next presidential election with impatience. We are at an historic moment, at a turning point. When you listen to Bush's speech in Warsaw, when you see the positions he takes in Madrid, these are speeches which are not explicitly hostile to the European Union, but which propose other political agendas, such that all efforts of American diplomacy consist in dividing Europeans. The Europeans divide all by themselves, also. Iraq caused a rift. Will they overcome these divisions? I think that the current American government will do its best to maintain them. French policy also, if it continues to rejoice when America falls on its face. But at the same time, if Bush continues to dictate the rules all by himself, he will end up encouraging anyone who believes that only a strong Europe will be able to defend its own interests, because Washington no longer bothers to take them into consideration. There are two factions today: those who contend that the current crisis is due to Bush's policies and that should change come to Washington, we will have the opportunity to make amends; and those who believe that the divide is concurrent with the history of the two continents. I belong to the first group: I hope that other American governments will correct these mistakes, just as other French governments will arrive at another concept of European identity, which will not necessarily assert itself against the United States as Jacques Chirac believes. Europeans have enough at stake among themselves, enough obstacles to overcome, that they don't need an outside enemy. Yesterday it was the Soviet Union. It would be mad to think that today's enemy might be the United States. It would be a total misinterpretation of history. But on the part of the US, I also believe it is a misinterpretation to oppose the building of the European Union, which would be a strong factor in promoting prosperity and stability.

WELLS: Amen.

COLOMBANI: Alleluia!

4
America and France, the Dream versus Reality

America fascinates just as much as it exasperates. France seduces as much as it inspires indifference. On both sides, idealized pictures mix illusion and fantasy. In the dream versus reality, both Americanophilia and Francophilia establish the beloved country, if not as a model, at least as an example or source of inspiration. The recent friction, however, should not make us lose sight of the fact that Americanophilia and Francophilia are still realities deeply rooted in French and American society.

The United States has always fascinated the French. While Chateaubriand thought he had found a pure race on the new continent, others, such as de Tocqueville, Jules Verne, and Georges Duhamel, perceived with either dread or enthusiasm that America was the laboratory of the future. Freedom and modernism, economic prosperity, the "American way of life," the myth of the "self-made man," a certain simplicity in social relationships coming from the relaxed, cordial attitude and the cosmopolitan mix of American society, all form the attractive image of the United States which haunts the French imagination.

Americans on, the other hand, have long suffered from an inferiority complex regarding the country that is the symbol of good taste, refinement and Culture with a capital C, where the art of living is almost a national sport. Lafayette's homeland still inspires profound admiration among a certain part of the American population. In another era, Thomas Jefferson went so far as to declare, "Every man has two countries, his own and France." Can anyone imagine a more profound expression of affection?

"In a certain way," Denis Lacorne has written, "the history of French-American relations is also the history of fluctuating opinion regarding the United States. After waves of infatuation rising suddenly and strongly, come waves of rejection just as sudden and exaggerated, as if public opinion could only find balance in continually swinging."[42] As a result, the unstable balance, the permanent tension between feelings and contradictory opinions, should be examined carefully. To what extent can one talk about Americanophilia and Francophilia? How can one explain the attraction exercised by both France and the United States? And on the other hand, what are the failings, real or imagined, attributed to both nations? Love and hate both feed on illusion. French-American relations do not escape that rule.

COLOMBANI: I am not at all sure that we can talk about Americanophilia in France as being equal to the current anti-Americanism. Nevertheless, for democrats, America is a model. In France, we always need to categorize things in order to differentiate the pure from the impure. The republicans are pure and the democrats are impure, according to the famous definition established by Regis Debray—a definition which might lead one to the conclusion that democracy is not republican, and that the Republic is not democratic. That's logical enough, since the national-republican sentiment dominating media and intellectual spheres today claims its origins lie in the Republic, which in France is consular. France bears the mark of the Consulat[43] much more than that of the monarchy of the Ancien Regime. Bonaparte as first consul still leaves his mark on the France of the 21st century. At any rate, this distinction between democrat and republican covers the split, albeit in a simplified manner, between partisans and opponents of the American model. The republicans feel they are capable of assuming their republican identity without American contamination, whereas the democrats—if you believe Regis Debray—are totally committed to, if not corrupted by, the American model.

Still, today, this democratic movement, which takes its source in the writings of de Tocqueville, nourishes all of French democratic life. The Tocquevillian sentiment in French society claims America as the place where both democratic experimentation and the realization of the democratic model occurred. The de Tocquevillian heritage is inspiration for the liberal right, rather than the Gaullist or nationalist right, but it is also very present in the left, for the French social-democrat movement leans more naturally towards the United States than communism. The social-democratic movement is *atlanticist*.[44] It's interesting to note that even the word "atlanticism," which should represent both a way of living a certain community of spirit and a community of interests shared with America, is considered a sin in France, and almost an insult. When you call someone an *atlanticist*, you are insulting him. During the presidential campaign of 1965, de Gaulle and his partisans denounced "the American party," thereby censuring the candidacy of Jean Lecanuet of the French Christian-Democratic party. And yet, the liberal right, Christian-Democrats, and reformist left, have always seen elements of progress in Europe stemming from the evolution of American society. The Fourth Republic, dominated by Socialists and Christian-Democrats— their alliance in Europe produced the Treaty of Rome—was ridiculed, denounced and ultimately beaten, namely because it was reputed to be atlanticist, that is, committed to the US. And in the 70s, a party on the left that was allied to both the Gaullists and communists, actually formed a "Committee against a German-American Europe." You have to bear in mind that categorization and historic given in order to understand how the French see the US, i.e., that America has been used as an internal political weapon against the reformist left.

Now let's look at the French elite. And the elite of the elite, who used to pray that their children went to ENA (Ecole Nationale de l'Administration) ten or fifteen years ago, and who are now sending their children to the United States. That, by definition, is selection by economics, which bypasses the egalitarianism of the French system, because in order to send your children to the United States, having money becomes the discriminatory barrier. At the same time, the model of the French elite lies not far from internalizing the idea of an "old" Europe in contrast to a "young" America. That ranges from summer camps in Vermont, to summer school in universities, and even finishing a degree. Today, graduating from MIT or another prestigious American university may not be as valued by the French elite as completing the Ecole Polytechnique, Ecole Centrale, or ENA, but it is recognized as an indispensable part of the experience of a graduate from a top school. Concurrently, the French people are very suspicious of this process of education that reproduces a closed elite. This suspicion enhances a strong resentment towards that elite. It would not be absurd to believe that, in turn, this discontent is responsible for some of the anti-American sentiment, since the United States has become the training ground for the unattainable elite.

The same goes for our intellectuals. Their creativity seems to me somehow related to the length of their stay in American universities. In fact, how could it be any other way? The Renaissance could only be conceived through the development of exchanges between universities all over Europe. It is the same now on both sides of the Atlantic. Which proves that French debates on

America are neither exempt from ulterior political motives, or from a hefty dose of hypocrisy. On the other hand, popular culture is a factor bringing us closer together. I am talking less about an American model and more about a common cultural bath, rich with multiple contributions. Through music that has African as well as Latino-American or North African roots; through television, which has created common standards, so that an American in Paris doesn't feel homesick. He can follow his favorite TV series here, usually in English. It is true that most of these series are high quality, as if the authors, their creativity being stifled by Hollywood, have turned to television instead.

If you ask me, the ambivalence of the French feeling of love/hate, has another explanation. France both admires and detests seeing the extension of what it used to be reflected in the US today, i.e., your succeeding in ambitions that used to be ours. The United States is the perpetuation of the model of the universal Republic that France has never stopped pursuing. Basically, what we envy in the United States, is what we would still like to be today. But we never should have lost at Waterloo....

As for Mitterrand, he never deviated from the line that the Socialist movement had always followed. In 1982 and 1983, during the Euro-missile crisis when the big question was whether the Europeans would accept US retaliation to the installation of the Soviet SS20 missiles, it was he who said: "The missiles are to the East, the pacifists are to the West!" A strategic response to a strategic crisis: In fact, this was the beginning of the end of the USSR. In the same vein, Mitterrand supported George Bush Senior during the first Gulf War. What did he say? That France had to "take its place" among the allies. In spite of major and multiform opposition to that "American war," Mitterrand's teaching allowed a majority of French to rally around a policy which no one qualified as "atlanticist," but which to me, allowed France to preserve its leadership in Europe.

What was true of the socialists on a political level, was also true on other levels: take unions, for example. In the beginning in fact, Europe was built around two atlanticist pillars: the Christian-democrats and the social-democrats. Both had union ties. Today, the markers are no longer the same, as Bernard Thibault, leader of the CGT (Confederation Generale du Travail),[45] was hailed as leader at the Socialist Convention in Dijon. But that represents less of a conversion of French socialists from what remains of communism, than a conversion to reformism of the CGT, formerly the "drive belt" of the French Communist Party, the PCF (Parti Communist Francais), and today, a member of the Confederation Europeenne des Syndicats (European Confederation of Trade Unions). Before, the organic link between the Socialists and unions was forged by Force Ouvriére, a union created in 1947 to oppose the communist CGT. This union was created from start to finish by an American, Irving Brown, who came from the international branch of the AFL-CIO. He was a fascinating character, moreover, who played an important role in the events of May 1968, when he was called in for reinforcement... by the Gaullist Party.

WELLS: Of course, immediately after the war, the Communists had heroic stature in France, because they had been so vital to the Resistance and because, too, of the very great sacrifices made by the Soviet Union in fighting Hitler. Also, to many war-weary Frenchmen, communism seemed to offer both a means to reject the systems and values that had led to war, and a better, faster way to recover from it. By 1947 there was a lot of concern among American policymakers that France was about to be "lost" to communism. And so the Americans helped to arrange for an alternative union to the CGT, which was loyal to Stalinism and the Party. I have wondered at times, in fact, if Marc Blondel's[46] militancy today could be motivated in part by the CIA "blemish" on Force Ouvrière, though of course he describes himself as a friend of America and merely a loyal socialist.

As for the comfort zone here when Americans come, you know, of course, that we'll not stop with music and clothes and fast food. We want to take over your language, too. *Dieu soit remercié que l'Académie francaise est là pour vous protéger*—Thank God that the Academy Francaise is there to protect you! (That's a joke—all of it.)

The kind of Americanophilia I'd like to talk about is the "feel good" kind, the kind I have experienced quite a lot of in the quarter century I have lived in France. I can count on the fingers of one hand the incidents when I thought I was being "dissed" because I was American. You can't walk through Kennedy Airport without being able to top that in half an hour. I cited the example of a quite grand lady who always stayed at the Ritz when she was in France, who socialized with the grandest names in the *Bottin*[47] and, despite all that protective bubble, was made to feel insecure by a sales woman at Cartier and maîtres d'hôtel in three-star restaurants. I think this is something that was in her, and not in her experiences, and not in the French.

The first time I came to France it was with this *certaine idée des francais,* and I admit it wasn't a very positive one. I was anticipating a hard time from a people who had a reputation as unwelcoming. The reputation was quickly erased—I had the time of my life. I thought I had come home, in fact, and determined that I would come back. And I did "come home" in a very strong sense, because my wife and I have always loved our life here. Without loving America any less, I add, and without having any intention of "becoming French" in any way except as taxpayers.

I thought that this reputation had been forgotten. Every year practically there is a fresh list of books in America about Paris and France, all of them paeans and tributes and outpourings of deep and special feelings that Americans—many, though certainly not all—have for this country.

But with Iraq as the catalyst, America slipped into a mode of France-bashing more virulent than ever. And it was not limited to the Joe Six-pack America, or to Fox News and the Murdoch press. It became pervasive—*Vanity Fair*, certainly no right-wing publication, wrote about anti-Semitism here in a way that practically made Paris sound like Berlin on Kristallnacht; *The Washington Post* has featured a steady drumbeat of francophobic columnists; *The Atlantic Monthly* published a blurb linking Chirac and Osama.

That kind of vituperative, hateful France-bashing has certainly not been reciprocated in France. And in fact no one here has asked me for anything other than an occasional explanation of Bush's policies, and that in the context of my job as a journalist. The French are better able to distinguish between what the American government is doing, and what Americans are doing. In the United States we are much more likely to simplify, to turn our adversaries into our enemies, and to blame the French first, and the French government as only the highest manifestation of disloyalty and our own particular kind of *lèse majesté*, ingratitude.

Aside from wine, a few chefs, and a few great restaurants in a few big cities, there's no effective French lobby in the US. There's no French voting bloc, there's no Bastille Day Parade. French movies have no impact in the mass market—unless they're remade into American movies. And I guess we think that Michel Le Grand[48] is one of the greatest American popular composers. The assistance that France gave against the British during the American Revolution is now historical detail, not something that stirs patriotic breasts. Perhaps it's comparable to de Gaulle dismissing the role of the British SOE in rallying and maintaining the Resistance,[49] but we recite poems about our own Paul Revere and none about that outsider Lafayette. And de Tocqueville? Who's that? And who's Derrida? Barthes? Foucault?

M. Tout-le-Monde may know who these lights of modern intellectualism are, but I would bet that Joe Six-Pack has no clue. And if he found out he would dismiss them first not as intellectuals, but as Frenchmen.

You've touched on a lot of points, and as always with eloquence and intelligence. I'd like to go back to your references to America as a model for this republic and this democracy. In reality, we have nurtured one another in our republican aspirations and struggles. France and America are the world's two oldest republics, and though the American experience with republican democracy is a bit older than your own, and has been considerably more durable and stable, both were products of the same 18th century cauldron. (I like to say that ours is older because I am reminded so often by my French friends that ours is a "young" country, unlike the ancient civilization of France.)

It's easy to become maudlin when talking about the America that inspires democracies. It has inspired, of course, and continues to inspire. It fosters democracy because, well, because democracy is good for its beneficiaries. And because American democracy is good for the folks who live there, a lot of people make considerable efforts to do that. Something like 4,000 immigrants arrive every month, only a quarter of them legal.

Part of that is what I call the Berlin Wall effect. The Soviet Union was already a spent force when it collapsed, but it's also true that the revolution that began with the opening of the Berlin Wall was a media revolution, a sea change inspired by the media. Because it had been possible for a long time for East Berliners to see on television the lives that their cousins in the West enjoyed, and as that awareness grew it became a force that could not be stopped.

America also is that kind of model, because no matter how violent it appears from the outside, or how angry liberals may become under the current administration, or how cynical I may feel about it, America is a powerful magnet for people who live in deprivation, whether economic or political. We think that a magnet with that much pull should be not just a model but a paragon. Of course it is not. No country is. No model stands up to close scrutiny. The imperfections are not just present, but sometimes blinding.

Military power makes America another kind of model, because it isn't just copied—ultimately a model controls and directs. The US has the muscle, and it will throw punches. Hero worshippers don't like to be beaten up by their heroes. Because America is huge and powerful and throws its weight around, sometimes it becomes not a model at all, and certainly not a model that can be followed, because it is big and powerful.

I do not know to what extent that magnet is the thing that draws the French academics who go to recharge their batteries on American campuses. If it's deprivation they are escaping, that's certainly not apparent. But no doubt the same effect is present for them as for the students, the ones whose parents were *énarques*.[50] It is not that America is a better democracy than France, but America does offer more freedom and more opportunities. For some young Frenchmen, America is not the country of the *second* chance, but the country of the *first* chance, and of the preferred chance. And I think of my young mason, who couldn't be a farmer though that's what he wanted to be, because his father was a mason and he had to do what his father had done. He was a very good mason, and as I set about restoring my house I was glad that his father had been a mason. But it was puzzling, and saddening, too, to think that he saw his choices being so restricted.

Young Americans come to Europe, too, for study—prep school in the UK, a junior year in France or Italy to study art and culture. I hope that the experiences they have, whether in France or elsewhere, will help create an elite in my country that will be wiser about the world than their parents are. I hope they will gain not just in sophistication, but in common sense about the importance of international comity.

That was surely lacking in the disputes over Iraq, and that is too bad.

I said earlier that I didn't buy into the notion of "cultural imperialism," and I would like to explain myself. Culture, and mass culture especially, is a buyers market. People in France flock to American movies and watch American television and line up for American fast food because it's easy and available and because all those things enhance the notion of flexibility and adaptability. I may deplore that there's no Orson Welles in American cinema, that Ray Kroc[51] never dined at La Pyramide (assuming he didn't), or that William Paley[52] was so influential in American popular culture rather than André Malraux. But what's so wonderful about steak-frites? or Louis de Funes?[53] or those paintings for sale in Montmartre of waifs peeing?

Popular culture is *populaire*, for the people. And I say let them eat Big Macs. They line up for it here just as geese do for the *gavage*. There's no forced feeding involved. It's strictly a buyer's market.

I actually had not realized that the concept of atlanticism was regarded as negative in France—though I realize also that reaction is naïve, because the policy was developed by the British and the Americans and since the war has been dominated by the United States. But it is surprising because what we regard as atlanticism is really a community of values to which France certainly subscribes.

Atlanticism really boils down to peace and prosperity, to fall back on a cliché familiar from too many political speeches. But if not negatively viewed from the US, and if still important, it is declining as a policy muscle because more and more we look west. Our position on the Pacific Rim has been increasingly important, both because of the need for stability, as in places like the Korean Peninsula and Indonesia, and because of the democratic free-market trends in China. This Pacific community of values is also important—they are alliances where our leadership is still required and is not yet challenged as assertively as it has been recently in Europe. Asia is also important because of the vast workforce it provides to Western manufacturers, European as well as American, and its potential as a market.

America has tended to ignore Europe except perhaps to speak to Europe in a way that Chirac spoke to the central Europeans himself: "You're missing a good opportunity to keep quiet and to learn where you fit into this enterprise."

But back in this traditional transatlantic community of values, France and the United States play parallel and contrapuntal roles: We both think of ourselves as exceptions, and we both think of ourselves as repositories of universal truth and protectors of democratic values. It's curious, isn't it, that universal truth can have so much variance from one concept to another, from ours to yours. That leads to a lot of the cause for disagreement between us. In our exceptionalism, we see ourselves as singularly competent to save the world, and specifically tasked with doing so. George Washington instructed us: "The name of American, which belongs to you, in your national capacity, must always exalt the just pride of Patriotism.... It should be the highest ambition of every American to extend his views beyond himself, and to bear in mind that his conduct will not only affect himself, his country, and his immediate posterity; but that its influence may be co-extensive with the world, and stamp political happiness or misery on ages yet unborn."[54]

I'm surprised that in our current fervor we haven't adopted that as our Pledge of Allegiance—and there may be right-wing groups that advocate that we do so.

French exceptionalism is rather to resist American hegemony, to hold itself up as another beacon, "the other way," defending (in the words of Chirac) its independence and thereby drawing support from others who resist American policy. And that is the nub, isn't it? That is the crux of the issue between the two countries.

There is a perception in France that since the collapse of the Soviet Union, and as America has faced the insidious threat of terrorism, American administrations have abandoned traditional leadership, and shifted instead to a tough hegemony. On the other side of the ocean, there is a perception that France, feeling its prestige and position threatened in a world with a single superpower, and a single-minded superpower, is committed to resisting every international policy and initiative that America undertakes.

Neither perception is accurate. But until both sides move beyond those perceptions, the kind of conflict that Iraq came to represent is probably inevitable.

One of the questions that framed this discussion asks whether the American dream is only a mirage: Can an immigrant still rise from the bottom to the top? To push the question beyond the parameters you gave it: Hasn't the era of the "self-made man" been replaced by a traditional and dangerously anti-democratic plutocracy?

There are probably no Abraham Lincolns in America's future. Probably nobody else will be born in a log cabin and become president, if only because there are not so many log cabins any more. However, Bill Clinton gained the presidency from quite modest beginnings. There are many other 20th century examples— Harry Truman, Richard Nixon, Gerald Ford, Lyndon Johnson— that are far different from the Kennedys and Rockefellers in terms of wealth, or the Bushes in terms of nepotism

It is also possible, certainly, to rise to a considerable economic summit in the United States. I've met dozens of men who have arrived as immigrants without two nickels to rub together, as we say. There's even a club of men who rose from poverty to great wealth, named after Horatio Alger,[55] the fictional but prototypical rags-to-riches success story. It's like the image developed by Arthur Miller, when Willy Loman[56] talks wistfully about his brother going into the jungle with nothing and coming out with untold wealth.

That it is still possible to do that in the United States speaks again of the idea of the flexibility and the openness and opportunity.

You made an important point about money being discriminatory, and it's obvious that penury excludes a lot of Americans. But it is neither a systematic exclusion nor a closed system, the way a centralized country like France tends to be. France really is a club—and you can only be born into it. If you're not, you can become an associate member, but not a full member.

One of the reasons that ideas like affirmative action are so important to the American psyche—no matter how much they may be contested and resisted—but one of the reasons that they prevail finally is that they have helped to create opportunity. The image that Clinton gave us for diversity during his presidency was the statement that he wanted an administration that "looked like America"—men and women, blacks and whites, Hispanics and Asian Americans. Not a melting pot, but a rainbow.

There is now a very strong commitment to diversity in big American companies. The requirement was placed there by the courts, and enforced in some instances by boycotts and campaigns in the press to expose failures in diversity. But it took root and flourished, I think, because Americans are basically fair-play people.

I was frankly stunned to read something in *Le Figaro* recently quoting a member of the National Assembly about the issue of diversity in France—specifically it was the debate over headscarves that Islamic girls want to wear in school—and making a critical reference to "*la dérive américaine.*"[57] Meaning, I guess, that famous melting pot, or rainbow. What kind of "drift" is that, I wondered. What's so bad about a "drift" toward openness and opportunity? And how, by the way, does allowing the scarves challenge the principle of secularity? Or pose any threat to the state or to the other students? A lot of French kids probably wear chains with little crosses that are visible, and there's no dispute about that, nor should there be.

America's strength is based on what the Assemblyman thought of as "drift." The original question concerned how the United States could be changed for the better, and there are many, many ways. But of course America isn't based so much on changing itself as it is on starting over. It's the land of the New Deal, the Fair Deal.[58] People come there for that second chance. They want a break. And the ultimate strength of the country is the *dérive* that makes a break not just possible, but the norm.

COLOMBANI: There is indeed an ideal America; it's the US of Woodrow Wilson and Franklin Roosevelt. It's the America of the Kennedy myth, a vision both generous towards external affairs and more just on internal ones. That America comes closest to the model dominating Europe in the years following the Second World War, the years of reconstruction and progressive concretizing of the Welfare State. Where that Assemblyman saw a "drift," others—myself included—see the driving force and extraordinary energy that leads Americans to set goals, one more ambitious than the next. The entire social body seems to respond to the same goal, through mechanisms for absorbing the different waves of immigration, which make America the land of the second chance. America as the land of the new beginning for the disinherited, of Europe yesterday, of all continents today, is truly a reality. Moreover, this is true to such an extent that immigration will soon influence whether America—where Hispanic and Asian components are becoming so important—will or will not be composed of Europeans. Yesterday it meant refuge and promise for famine-stricken Europe: Ireland, Italy. Today it is the land chosen by those fleeing the absence of freedom at home. True or false, the idea that America is the land of liberty is perpetuated. The land of Montesquieu was never really in competition with you for that title, after two imperial periods and the sinister episode of Vichy. Europe, which is welded together around the Declaration of the Rights of Man, would do better to try to regain the title, in an age where it is tempted to cut itself off from the rest of the world. It is building the Union and closing its borders.

The difficulty in our relations with the United States also comes from a reality that is difficult to accept: The evolutions that mark the United States are felt in Europe, but with a time lag. This should, however, allow us to anticipate and attempt better control here than is exercised in the US, especially with regards to the way inequality sets in. I would not say that the United States sets an example for France, nor is it a counter-example; but it is a continent in movement that incites us to never relax our own efforts. Intellectual and financial efforts, that is. To think that Europe only allots 1.9% of its gross national product to research, as opposed to 2.8% in the US. Where there are 5.4 researchers per 1000 in Europe, there are 8.08 in the United States! We can only imagine the scientific and technological drain that lies in wait for Europe, where, at the height of the 90s, one could have imagined that potentially Europe was on the same level as the US in these areas. Money and freedom: that's what draws scientists from all over the world to the United States.

These areas are where the American model is particularly seductive and influential to our elite. These are sectors of the European economy which exist independently of the world economy, where leaders refer continually to the American model. They tend to explain our difficulties, our delays, by the fact that we don't import recipes from across the Atlantic quickly enough. From this viewpoint, the great debate currently is about the 35-hour work week. This reform symbolizes a social model where free time is an important concept, whereas in the United States the work ethic persists. The relationship to earned rights is another component of the European model. Such are the elements obviously under debate in the global economic spheres of our two countries. There, too, the American model is on the side of the oppressor, on the side of the employer as the caricature boss who would like to impose *"cadence infernales"*—hellish schedules—have total freedom to fire, to withdraw benefits, and so on. In fact, in our public lives, there are two foils, two alibis that politicians use and abuse. The first is to nationalize the successes of a government and Europeanize its failures: if things go well, it's thanks to Paris; if things go badly, it's Brussels' fault! The second is to explain that when social problems arise, they are always due to the economic liberalism of the American way of life. This is a complete reversal of the years immediately following the war. In one of his best films, *Holidays,* Jacques Tati plays the role of a postman in France of the 50s, who claims to deliver mail in a modern way—*à l'americaine*. Today, according to dominating imagery, he wouldn't be modernizing, he would be fired—*à l'americaine!*

Let's get to what is exasperating about America. There are two things: the reverse side of the American social model, and, above all, the violence. America was forged in violence, in the violence generated by immigration, and slavery, which must not be forgotten. Look at Scorsese's film, *Gangs of New York*. He conjures up the memory of the terrible atmosphere during the 19th century. It's a time of civil war, a component of the American nation. One question must be asked: Is the model for this violence not the conquest of the West? The conquest of the West was nothing more than what the US accused us of—rightly so—applied to their own territory, namely, colonization. America itself is a land of internal colonization and the extermination of the Indians. Europe has known its own wars of secession, civil wars, world wars and even the immense mass grave that the territory known as the "Old World" became twice in this century. As far as violence is concerned, we have pioneers and experts.

Today however, what distinguishes us from America— but for how long?—is your capacity to accept violence and to integrate violence into your society. The last film which won at the Cannes Festival, *Elephant*, bears witness to this fact, having been directly inspired by the killing at Columbine High School in the United States.

Then there is the reverse of America's social model. An example? The health insurance reform project presented by Hillary Clinton and its failure—proof that America's motivating forces are profoundly reactionary, to our eyes, in the sense that for us, the reaction constituted a synonym for social regression.

Another thing is the fact that in the American social model, employment is the factor used for systematic adjustment. When Boeing has problems, they fire 10,000, 15,000 employees. At the same time, this society has turned competition into its motivating force. Competition is an extraordinary constraint that never lets up. It brings true toughness to social interaction that rapidly leads to violence. Such is, albeit in a summarily Marxist nutshell, the dominating perception of American social reality in Europe and France.

Deep down, the part of America that exasperates most is the part setting President Wilson apart from President Roosevelt. It is a period that excites us—Chicago in the 1920s and 30s, for example, was legendary and fascinating. Let it be said in passing that Chicago of that time is quite like Moscow of today, which the whole world hates. At the end of the 20s, a realist writer close to the American socialist left, Sinclair Lewis, wrote an outstanding novel entitled *Babbitt*.[59] Babbitt was a small-time employer in the Mid-West, enjoying prosperity, hating the unions, workers, Blacks, presenting all the characteristics of the nouveau rich, and narrow-minded to begin with. At the time of the 1929 crisis, when J. Edgar Hoover was the ruthless head of the FBI, under a particularly limited Secretary of the Treasury, Andrew Mellon, the metaphor of "Babbitt" was used by the left to denounce the marriage of Wall Street to Main Street, of international finance to the most obtuse, petite bourgeoisie, of the lucre of New York finance to the provincialism of upstarts. These were the forces that the New Deal and the Second World War swept off the summit of American politics. These forces, kinds of Jehovah's Witnesses of the economy, refused to heal a sick society, screamed at Roosevelt's "Bolshevism," refused to defend democracy in Europe against the Nazis to whom they attributed certain virtues and with whom they did not dislike doing business, were responsible for one of the most resounding political bankruptcies of modern history. While on the contrary, Roosevelt incarnated the fundamental democratic values of the United States. Then the Cold War came along and eroded these same values once again, creating alliances against nature in the name of the fight against communism, opening the way to Reagan, his counter-revolution and the return of the pact between Wall Street and Main Street. His program: deregulation, obliteration of the State, and capital punishment.

For me, the admirable motivating force in America is its capacity to renew, progress, integrate. In the long run, it's progress that dominates. Even if Bush's fiscal program is nonsense. Too great a division of wealth will ultimately destroy the social fiber, unless—which is highly unlikely—America has a capacity to absorb such inequality, unless it is so permeated with inequality that it can in fact adjust to it, while waiting for better times. To go towards such distortion, hailing injustice as the order of the day in politics, seems unacceptable to me. One wonders how great the inequality must become before there is revolt! But, you may say, accounts will be rendered in the fall of 2004, when Bush will face the electorate.

WELLS: We have taxpayer revolts. I never understand why there are no taxpayer revolts in France, where the level of taxation is one of the highest in the world. The revolts here in France are for more taxes—because they are for higher benefits.

There are only two points I would add. On Hillary Clinton, as worthy as the idea was—becoming more so by the day when I read about medical costs—the momentum just wasn't there. And the Clintons handled it very badly. They made a fundamental mistake in not involving the medical profession more fully in the planning. She relied on the advice of lawyers—she's a lawyer, the president was a lawyer, all their advisers are lawyers, most of the people in government are lawyers. And yet doctors and patients were the ones to be affected. That was not politically savvy. But she's gotten a lot smarter since then, a whole lot smarter.

And the second point: I would certainly not argue with you about violence. The level of violence that Americans will tolerate in our society is puzzling and demoralizing. I say with cynic's humor that we are going to have to give every American a bazooka or a Howitzer because giving them all simple rifles and handguns is not enough. They need to upgrade to grenade launchers to protect themselves. It's an outrageous aspect about the United States that a Constitutional guarantee for revolution-aries to have muskets two centuries ago to protect themselves on the frontier now protects people who think they need assault rifles. But while *Gangs of New York* was a very good portrayal of vio-lence, it wasn't very good history.

COLOMBANI: We don't ask artists to remain true to history. We ask them to have blinding visions, to put their finger right where it hurts.

WELLS: Right. It's the fabulists of movie making who determine a lot of what we know about the world nowadays, and a lot of what the French know about us. Movies are an art, and art requires a willing suspension of disbelief. And that's harder with movies, which portray reality and therefore turn into reality. We can look at a painting by Francis Bacon and know it's one man's vision. But

when we look at a film by Stone or Scorsese, we think we're seeing history or reportage. Whether it's *Nightmare on Elm Street* or
Gangs of New York, people tend to believe what's on the screen
because they've seen it with their own eyes. Although they probably do not believe "Pleasantville."[60] We know more, or think we
do, about the Kennedy assassination from Oliver Stone than we
do from the facts of the case, because few of us have bothered to
read the facts—we didn't need to. We only needed to absorb all
the conspiracy theories of the last 40 years and see them confirmed by a film. And no doubt many of us will never be able to
think of the early days of America again without thinking about
The Gangs of New York. That may have been a brilliant film, but it
didn't tell you any more about New York 150 years ago than
Travis Bickle[61] of *Taxi Driver* told you about New York cabbies.

"Cultural imperialism" may distort French tastes and change
values, but it also distorts what is known about America, and
there's a cultural downside in the way America is portrayed on
the screen, big or little. That was driven home to me by a review
of *Gangs* in *Le Nouvel Observateur*, which said there was no surprise
that a country with such a violent past was so willing to start a
war in Iraq. Well, *touché*. Payback time for those of us who say
France is collaborationist-born and collaborationist-bred. *Touché*.

Of course, our movies reflect the fact that we ourselves don't
have a very positive image of America any more. We don't think
of our elected officials as Jimmy Stewart, or our soldiers as John
Wayne. Because of Vietnam, Watergate, the political assassina-
tions of the 60's, America has matured. We have learned the consequences of being very wrong—a lot of people would say that has
happened again in Iraq—and we have grown cynical. There was
an interlude, the Reagan years, when America was said to be
"back" again. But America will probably never be "back" to what
it was in the postwar years, when there was a genuine feeling that
America had saved the world, and a real pride in having done so.

Nevertheless, America is more than *Dallas* and *Bowling for Columbine*. It's also suburbs with green lawns and block parties in the cities and baseball games and a lot of people living quiet, satisfying lives.

COLOMBANI: Yes, it's also the reign of the middle classes, with a ten to fifteen year head start on the European continent. It is, at the same time, a motivating force for democratic life, since the cohesion of the middle classes, and the assurance of a social elevator within the classes, are the best guaranties that democracy can offer. But at the same time, the middle classes on both sides of the Atlantic resemble each other: their lifestyles, appetites are the same, their distractions are the same, their dreams the same. At the same time, the ideological reflexes are similar enough, albeit with the temptation to lean towards strict defense of their categorical interests, in Europe as well as the United States. The underside of the American middle class is also *American Beauty*, even if we owe this description of their shortcomings to Sam Mendes, a European director.

But in spite of all the wrongs and basic disagreements that exist between France and the US, you still continue to fascinate the French. I am not sure that the opposite is true. France, for the United States, has only been idealized by Walter Wells!

WELLS: Actually, I may have lived here too long and endured too many strikes to idealize France any more. And at this particular moment in history, there are probably not many Americans who think of France in an idealized way. Some detest France—we've been through that—but some do think of France as a repository of human rights, of civil liberties, of noble aspirations for mankind, of virtue. They think of France as advocate and practitioner of "good" policies as opposed to the "bad" or at least questionable policies that America the Arrogant, America the Ugly applies…except maybe when you go off exploding nuclear bombs or building nuclear power plants. The people who admire France most would disapprove of those policies.

Many Americans thought that Bush was totally wrong on Iraq, though some of them felt constrained to support the policy because it's basic to our culture to support our troops when their lives are at stake. Many Americans think that Bush and his advisers botched Iraq, that maybe France wasn't so wrong after all. Whether he botched it or not, with the wrong justification and bad planning, I'm not willing, myself, to bet against the administration's determination there.

But Americans do not think of France in the same way they think of their own country. We're frankly proud of being a superpower, the only remaining superpower, even if the power isn't always used well. On the other hand, we think that—how can I put this without causing offence?—that France is a pretender to much greater status than it possesses, and that France's mission is a pretentious one, self-assigned. It's as though France still hasn't dealt entirely with losing at Waterloo. And we are obsessive about it— absurdly obsessive. The Bush administration must take France and "Old Europe" very seriously indeed to let their preoccupation with the French determine so many of their words and deeds.

What Americans do have strong feelings about and respect for is France as a super *cultural* power.

What is best and most enduring about France in the American experience is that it is the Everest of high culture and *art de vivre*— museums, style, the beauty and elegance in this marvelous country, with fabulous wines and excellent food and three-hour lunches. Or just the delicious pleasure of spending an hour reading the paper at an outdoor café. There's a concern for comfort and for well being here that's reflected not just in the aesthetics but in the French social structure as well. The standard of living in France is much higher across the board than it is in the United States,

I think, and that gets at another aspect of France that I admire a great deal. Unlike the United States—a society that is fundamentally and unabashedly every man for himself—France is a caring society. *Solidarité* is palpable here, sometimes frustratingly so, as in the case of retirement at 55 in certain sectors, which contributes to an unreasonable, counter-productive tax burden.

Of course, that *solidarité* takes its form in a providential state—*civisme* is pretty well limited to demands that the state do something to help the disadvantaged, or to make the weather cooler. But as for the application of that *solidarité* at a personal level, *touches pas à ma poche, ni à mes jours fériés.*[62]

"Sauve qui peut"[63] is a French expression, though the instinct is multicultural.

5
To Renew the Transatlantic Alliance

During the second half of 2003, French-American relations calmed down. In June, 2003, at the G8 Summit in Evian, President George W. Bush declared: "I am not angry with France. Among allies, you may have differences, but what brings the US and Europe closer together is infinitely more important.[64] Two days later, the American and French presidents were shaking hands. Since the end of the war, all votes by the Security Council have been unanimous, including Resolution 1511, which ratified America's presence in Iraq. But this desire to calm things down, this attitude of "responsibility and lucidity," in the words of Dominique de Villepin, can dissipate neither the accumulated resentment, nor the serious lack of confidence dividing the two nations.

To be sure, the threat of sanctions against France no longer seems to be on the agenda. Even during the worst moments of the Iraqi crisis the dialogue never ceased and France never stopped cooperating with the United States. But one may well doubt that the passing of time and demonstrations of good faith will be sufficient to restore French-American relations, unless, of course, you may be satisfied with a façade. Changing leadership would certainly facilitate things, but a disagreement of this magnitude is not merely a misunderstanding among individual men. The stakes are greater than that. In the strategic reorganization currently underway, what place is the United States reserving for its European allies? Are they being relegated to a lesser role in order to further an alliance with Russia? Could Islamic terrorism bring the West together in a united strategy, as it was united in the face of the Communist threat? What remains of the common vision of the world, on which the foundations of a renewed French-American alliance may be laid?

COLOMBANI: What will become of our relations and beyond that, how will the relations between Europe and the United States evolve? As far as we're concerned, the most widespread impression is this: In order for our countries to get back on the right track, the leaders must change. In that respect, we will have a first indication in 2004 during the American presidential election, where one of the issues will be security outside of the US. At the same time, there will be a first and perhaps last assessment of Bush Jr. by American voters. Imagine, for a moment, that Bush is beaten—would that be enough? Are we not living with the illusion that all we need is for Bush to lose for everything to sort itself out?

To be sure, one cannot deny that official French circles, through their own rhetoric, have, little by little, engendered the notion in French public opinion that America is the problem, that the world would be much better off if Bush were not at the helm. This is probably true, but at the same time, a shift is taking place in the hierarchy of priorities. After all, when the US insists that we must exert pressure on Hamas, and that in order to reach them, you must go through Damascus, they are not wrong. When the French argue that the US is wrong, they are being hypocritical. France is merely trying to preserve its relations with Damascus, as it was trying to preserve its relations with Baghdad.

We are not trying to hide that fact. However, it seems to me that the true rift lies elsewhere. We have to go back to the basis for the Euro-American relationship.

Let's not forget that we are living in important times. This is a moment like none other, where we have the vague feeling that everything could fall into confusion, where everything is in movement, as if we are walking through quicksand. A certain anxiety pervades, as everyone realizes that at the end of this era a New World order will be established in which no one, at present, knows where the focal point will be. As at the turn of the last century, we are experiencing a complete upset of the geopolitical balance of the planet. But in the 20th century, the planet was not durably rebuilt until two world wars passed. We worry that the multipolar world currently being developed is being constructed in violence and terror. We are now confronted with the perspective of long years of war against a terrorism claiming to be militantly Islamist—a terrorism with the intention of attacking all democracies, even within the confines of the Arab-Muslim world, attacking any and all who dream of freedom.

In any case, the situation effecting us today is unique and dangerous in that it is leading Europe and America away from one another, precisely at a time when circumstances should bring them closer together in order to renew vital solidarity.

This is true, of course, only if one believes that democracy may be threatened by global terrorism.

The most immediately visible cause of the division on both sides of the Atlantic has a name: Iraq. Europe said no to the war in Iraq. While American and British troops moved into the regions surrounding Iraq, European public opinion stood fast in its refusal to partake in any military intervention to oust Saddam Hussein from Baghdad. This given did not weigh in the decision of the United States. Wrongly so. It was dangerous not to seek a prior agreement. Events subsequently proved that. For months on end, three positions were expressed in Europe by the governments of the three main countries in the European Union. On one end of the spectrum is Tony Blair ("Use the United Nations to validate the war!"). On the other end is Gerhard Schröeder ("With or without the UN, no to war!"). And in the middle is Jacques Chirac ("Use the UN to prevent war!"). But as time passed, it appeared that the German Chancellor best expressed a more resistant European opinion: Nearly 60 percent of the British and more than 70 percent of the French felt that war in Iraq was unjustified, with or without the green light of the UN. All in all, the European tide had turned, and on the crest of the wave came strong support from Pope John Paul II. Chirac rose to the occasion by vetoing the resolution. Like Chirac, European opinion was not convinced of the immediate danger of Saddam Hussein. Europe didn't believe the proof of Iraq's implication in terrorist movements any more than it believed the evidence that Baghdad was ready to deploy weapons of mass destruction against the United States or its neighbors. For Europe, that was up to George W. Bush to prove. The fact that proof is long in coming makes things worse between America and Europe.

WELLS: If we have learned anything from the Bush administration's Wild West approach in Iraq, it is that marching in with guns blazing might not be the best way of achieving the goal. Bush the father apparently failed to teach Bush the son that in pursuing a strategy that's vital to your interests, the wider the coalition the more effective the effort. "United we stand," as Americans were once fond of saying. Bush seems to have replaced that with chest pounding and a Tarzan yell.

But I think we learned something from the French-led opposition to America's problematic Iraq strategy, and I hope that Chirac and Villepin learned something, too. I learned from a wise friend, a lawyer, that there are two approaches to negotiation.

There's the kind you have every day with your wife. And while it's important to win those negotiations, at least some of the time, it's more important to remain married. And then there's the kind of negotiation you have when the marriage is irreparably over. There's nothing to preserve, and you want to win at all costs, because losing is going to cost dearly. The Chirac and Villepin performance was the second kind of negotiation. And then they were stunned when the divorce came through. The American press—even its most liberal mainstream voice, *The New York Times* editorial page—is still running pieces about the French as the enemy. So while I hope the Americans learned something about the need for allies, I hope the French learned something about holding onto friends. Getting to "yes" doesn't always have to mean starting with "no."

COLOMBANI: But besides the immediate disagreement, what are the more profound reasons for this historic rift, the reasons making Europe and America move further apart at perhaps the worst possible moment?

The objective factors for the distancing are based on two observations. First, today's Europe, and the European Union now being built, is no longer the Europe of the West. This is a direct consequence of the fall of the Berlin Wall and of the coming of the Eastern bloc countries to this community of democracies. Soon, with the growth of the European Union, the center of the Old World will be moved to the East. The best example of this is the displacing of the German Federal capital from Bonn to Berlin. A major preoccupation of the European Union is its opening to the East. And the next debate for the Union will be to determine if Turkey may join, hence turning once again towards the East. This major geographical consideration will undoubtedly prompt Europe to redefine itself and to develop as a European entity, no longer a Europe of the West. This is a fundamental change.

Secondly, the United States itself is being forced—like it or not—to adopt reasoning that George Bush's predecessors in the White House dubbed "hemispheric." And like it or not, American leaders are called upon day after day to deal with the collapse of Argentina, Uruguay, Bolivia or even Brazil—even though Bolivia is already the third largest recipient of American military aid. The construction of NAFTA—the North American common market—also contributed to this hemispheric concept, whereas George Bush's platform has the US adhering more and more to a protectionist philosophy. This can already be seen in certain sectors, such as agriculture, metallurgy, aeronautics. This attitude poses serious problems for Europe, as for most parts of the world. Two geographical concepts are at work, to which we must add purely subjective elements. It would take forever to make an inventory of all the possible resentments people might harbor on either side of the Atlantic. We mentioned anti-Americanism, which in spite of precautions taken by our leaders, seems to have become the official line, and we have discussed the return of anti-French sentiment in the United States.

We could also mention Spain, Italy and Greece, three countries that lived under dictatorships supported by the United States in the name of fighting the communist threat. The resentment in each of these countries may not be highly visible, but it is no less profound. Or we might bring up the head-on, ideological opposition of Ronald Reagan to the social-democratic model dear to all of the democracies of Northern Europe. Or, finally and more recently, we might evoke the slow detaching of German public opinion from an America that it understands less and less. One must also take into account the evolution of American society. As Alain Minc wrote in *Le Monde*, "with Hindus taking the place of Jews, the Chinese substituting for 'WASPs,' and Hispanics replacing the Irish Catholics, how can one imagine that Europe remain the 'alma mater' of America?" It's a provocative way to highlight the fact that in the long run, the new America in gestation will develop a value system that will be even further from that of the Europeans.

All these givens were already in place before September 11, 2001. Reason or even wisdom should have brought America and Europe closer together. The heavy consequences of the division promptly took over again, as if September 11th and its immediate aftermath were merely a parenthesis. Ultimately, it was as if both countries wanted to act as though nothing had transpired. This return to square one even has a date: It occurred when George Bush made his "Axis of evil" speech,[65] designating the three links in the chain as Iraq, Iran and North Korea. The hostile European reaction to this speech—that of Chris Patten, Joschka Fischer and Hubert Vedrine—indicates clearly that there is a "before" and "after."

Before: The world is in shock after the attacks of September 11. With the exception of a handful of ultra–left wing intellectuals, few voices rise up to contest the legitimacy of the military operations in Afghanistan that were quickly decided upon, and quickly concluded by the departure of the Talibans.

After: It is, precisely, an "after," not an aftermath. Instead of pursuing the terrorists where they were or still are; instead of concentrating on the strategic interest dwelling in the region of Afghanistan (as it is very likely that the fate of the war against terrorism lies in Pakistan and more specifically in Karachi, which is the veritable headquarters of Al-Qaida), George Bush came quickly back to his electoral campaign promise. "I have decided," he decreed, "Saddam must leave." How better to describe to the rest of the world this return to a strictly US-centric vision of international affairs, then by this retreat to a strategic, ideological perspective ruled only by national interests as defined by the Pentagon? A return to an ideological policy dominated by hostility to Bill Clinton and the denouncing—particularly by Ms. Rice— of his penchant for "multilateralism."

In fact, there does exist a complex of forces in the US born from the Cold War. Eisenhower himself denounced it in his last speech on the "military-industrial complex," which today might be renamed "security-industrial." These are, in any order: the police; judges who are overly attached to capital punishment, of which the emblamatic figure is Attorney General John Ashcroft; a system of wire-tapping, capable of capturing every detail of a board meeting in a European aeronautic company, but incapable of decoding in a timely fashion conversations between members of Al-Qaida preparing an attack; and special forces like those that went into Afghanistan. All in all, this complex is influenced, ideologically speaking, by the American far right. Its reinforcement is disturbing. Its influence seems to be growing. Didn't Colin Powell himself, in his memoirs, state that he almost considered the current Vice President, Dick Cheney, or someone like Richard Perle, to be true representatives of the far right?

To a strict definition of national interests bound to American electoral imperatives, we must add two strong givens that contribute today and will continue to contribute tomorrow to the rift between America and Europe. On the one hand weighs the choice of a privileged alliance with Russia. Evidently George W. Bush has chosen to make Vladimir Putin his privileged ally, even though Putin decided to move progressively away from the democratic evolution underway in Russia. This move ranges from methods employed by the Red Army in Chechnya, to the slow and unrelenting gnawing away at freedoms that make some observers feel we are watching a "re-Sovietizing" of the system. And to this new Washington-Moscow "axis," we may add a very offensive concept of NATO. In the eyes of the US, this old and yet still current organization for defense is progressively becoming an instrument destined to provide a framework for the former countries of Eastern Europe—and why not even Russia tomorrow?—allowing them to bypass or neutralize the goals of the European Union.

To speak plainly, like George W. Bush, I would like to use an image. The British surely remember what Lord Ismay said of a budding NATO: "Keep the Yanks in; keep the Russians out; keep the Germans down." In my opinion, George Bush is not far from substituting his own formula: "Keep the Yanks out; keep the Russians in and keep the Europeans down."

In other words, in a new distribution of roles, let Washington and Moscow determine the fate of Europe among themselves at precisely the time when Europe should be deciding for itself. Not that it should go against the US, but remain alongside it—on the condition that, according to the very apt words of Joshka Fisher, Europeans be "partners" of the US and not "satellites." A wish, you might think, as to date no power, nor even influence, in Europe has provided the basis for such a partnership. For the moment in fact, all we see is a divided Europe. And neither Blair, nor Chirac (without coming to blows), knew how, or were able to deflect the American decision in time.

COLOMBANI: Let's get back to the heart of the problem—terrorism. This is a movement that has been formed with the purpose of "killing crusaders and Jews," as well as seeking to block any democratic process within the Arab-Muslim world. Perhaps there is an unacknowledged European attitude that a little complacency might allow Europe to go unnoticed. If that is the case, they are wrong.

Given the situation today, let's recall those who originally founded the cohesion between Europe and the United States. This comes down to two historic figures: Keynes and Kennan. Keynes[66] is the man who inspired policies for development used on both sides of the Atlantic, adopting a model serving the "social" and "liberal" aspects of qualityequally. Kennan[67] was the Undersecretary of State who invented the idea of "containment" to counter Soviet expansion. In its place, George Bush and Donald Rumsfeld propose the duo "protectionism and pre-emptive war." We have to hope that on both sides of the Atlantic, partisans of development and containment get back on top. This implies returning to an sufficiently powerful awareness of interdependence, that development once again becomes a transatlantic priority.

We also have to reinvent strategic doctrines that will bind our common interests together. It's up to the Europeans to create these. When Chirac puts forward the concept of a multipolar world, he is making a statement more than elaborating a doctrine. In the same vein, when Blair contradicts this vision of a multipolar world, he is describing British politics more than evoking a strategic doctrine capable of responding to the emergencies of the times: the fight against terrorism and the promotion of democracy. I have the feeling that both sides have broken down. We have broken down in politics and in alternative doctrines that would allow us to start up again on a healthy basis.

WELLS: The policy of containment did not spring full blown with George Kennan's famous 1947 "X Letter."[68] It evolved as the complications of the post-war world became clear. The Soviet Union posed a growing threat to Western values and stability, and it's unthinkable that having just fought the biggest and deadliest war ever, and having fought two world wars almost within a single generation, there would not have been every possible effort made to avoid another. Happily, the alliance to shield the West accomplished its purpose, even in the face of sometimes frequent bickering between America and its European allies.

Today the threat to our stability and values has been convincingly identified as global terrorism carried out by violent Islamism. The present impasse derives from the attack on America in September 2001. That Saddam Hussein apparently had nothing to do with 9/11 became almost—and perhaps stupidly—immaterial to the Iraq adventure. This administration became convinced that it's all the same poisonous atmosphere, the same fetid incubator. Saddam's Iraq was seen as the linchpin: Remove him, and begin eliminating the poison, begin clearing the way for a solution in Israel and facing up to the restive militancy in the Arab world.

This is the new destabilizing influence in our world, and at some point—probably, regrettably, after another series of horrendous attacks—we will eventually come to agree about that enough to settle on a true multilateral strategy for dealing with it. It would be fatally absurd to think that an alliance will not be essential to the strategy.

But back to the point: The kind of terrorism that has turned into a global threat is a calculated strategy in a perverted, desperate cause. And like many causes that turn perverted and desperate, it is rooted in something that is nevertheless comprehensible and reasonable: I see that idea as Islamic validation in a world that—it seems to the violent, political Islamists—seeks only to wall them off, banish them, kill their leaders with pinpoint missile strikes, and, now, destroy the governments of Islamic countries. In their minds, there's no issue whatsoever of justified retaliation against these targets for totally justifiable reasons. The fault is all on the side of the West.

Further, the Islamist cause is not time-sensitive—eternity is their frame of reference, and they also have the motivation of martyrdom. The only way they can see to escape the desperate morass they're trapped in is to die, and if you die as a martyr to the cause, then that's the ticket, they believe. That's the keys to the kingdom.

The mixture is a deadly cocktail, and in standing up to that mixture, our emotional and psychological resources are stretched as thin as America's military resources may be stretched in overcoming Iraqi resistance and reconstructing the country.

The very nature of terrorism makes it obvious that a strong and determined alliance will be necessary to resist it. But we— the alliance that has presided over peace and prosperity for the last half century—haven't started out that way. We haven't agreed on the nature of the threat, we haven't agreed on the strategy for dealing with it, we haven't agreed on our goals, and even within the Bush administration, apparently, we haven't agreed that Iraq figures materially in the terrorist threat.

Obviously, the old Western alliance has to come together again, and it has to expand to every nation that might get targeted. Perhaps the difficulties that the American administration is having in pacifying Iraq will help to accomplish that. The answer will depend on whether the Americans are arrogant and demanding as they seek help, or more reasonable in their approach now than they were when they walked away from the UN. And it depends, too, upon whether Chirac and Villepin now feel this marriage is worth saving after all. It's clear—it takes no crystal ball—that if the French are as willful in expressing their opposition this time around, it won't lead to a divorce, but a burial.

As for combating terrorism, it's clear—if current intelligence is accurate, and maybe again that's a big "if"—it's clear from the way that terrorist forces have poured into Iraq, battling the American and British troops but more significantly targeting the UN and the new Iraqi leadership, that this is as important a testing ground as Afghanistan was. George Bush himself acknowledges now that the war didn't end on May 1, but the word "quagmire" is one that the American administration chokes on. "Children went to school today," says Condoleezza Rice blithely, when asked about the problems that get the headlines. We are a long way from the scale of Vietnam—a decade's involvement, 50,000 American lives. But if this isn't a quagmire in the making, I'd like to know what it is? It's sure as hell not life in Pleasantville, as Ms. Rice seemed to want to focus on. The casualties are just one of many signs of a growing and effective resistance, even insurgency. Laser-guided missiles and smart bombs aren't so effective against the kind of resistance that Saddam Hussein told the world to expect. We all dismissed those warnings as more of Saddam's exaggerated rhetoric, but it appears that while he was faking the WMD, he wasn't lying about setting a trap.

Because of the nature of terrorism, containment alone will not be a sufficient strategy—though don't forget, containment wasn't just talk. A key element of the containment policy as it evolved was that communism would be stopped only where it met "unanswerable force."[69] And don't forget either that containment was anathema to conservative America. Republicans waged political war on the idea from the beginning, identifying it with appeasement—as they have again identified the French arguments in the UN as appeasement—and calling for a "crusade" to liberate the peoples enslaved by "godless communism" (though actually the Eisenhower and Nixon administrations were skilled practitioners of the Kennan policy they condemned in their speeches).

The concept expressed in Kennan's phrase "unanswerable force" is again the intended bulwark of the American policy for dealing with terrorism—even though terrorism is too scattershot and terrorists are too prone to independent initiative for containment to be 100 percent effective. There will have to be a new kind of containment applying a new kind of "unanswerable force." That implies tactics—"shock and awe" tactics—that can convincingly demonstrate to the strategists of this violence that their cause is at risk even more than they are themselves. That means a willingness to use warfare, including pre-emptively, perhaps even unilaterally.

Comparatively, as evil as it often was, communism was not devoid of reasonableness. America may have hated communism and its methods, but it was containable. What evolved on both sides was MAD—"mutual assured destruction"—but it wasn't as insane, maybe, as it appeared. Both sides knew that the principal enemy would never launch nuclear weapons. That's not an assumption we'll ever be able to make about Osama bin Laden, or about his disciples.

What has changed also—and this is quite significant —is that America cannot offer its shining shield against the new threat in the way our nuclear umbrella offered protection. It has nothing to bargain with—little *donné-donnant*.[70]

So we find ourselves deeply disoriented. The "new world order"[71] turned out even scarier than the old world order, and it has imposed the steepest possible learning curve in a frightening environment. Understanding the threat, understanding our vulnerability, developing a strategy for dealing with it, and creating a new interdependence, are all on the agenda. That's quite a challenge, and the enormity is even more daunting when you think also about how mediocre our leadership is in Bush and Chirac.

So will we change it? I am not a political optimist. Ours is a world in which the electorate tends to choose a candidate out of expediency, and the officials we elect choose tactics and strategy out of expediency. So despite the problems that Bush now faces—and they are growing by the day—I frankly do not expect him to be defeated next year. The United States government may face a mushrooming deficit, but the Bush re-election campaign faces none at all. It is not too far off base to say that Bush has practically unlimited resources for the re-election campaign. Not just money, but a dynamic and effective re-election machine that is gearing up to spin the situation in Iraq ("the children went to school today") into something that's palatable, even if they can't quite proclaim victory. Besides being reminded that "the children went to school today," the effort to rebuild Iraq is equated to the Marshall Plan, which of course means the war there is equated to World War II, fought most memorably in Old Europe. This spin cycle is transparent, but moving fast. By the time the campaign is over, in fact, France risks being demonized again, and particularly if Chirac continues to demonstrate that he likes the divorce.

It's far from clear who the Democratic candidate will be, and a lot can happen in a year, but the odds will be against the Democrat. He will get the nomination after a long bruising fight, so the party will be even weaker than it is—and he won't have enough money to match Bush. As I say, I am not a political optimist.

Unlike Tony Blair (the best of the lot, the only leader who rises above mediocrity), one of the things Bush will not have to demonstrate in his campaign is that America was right in going to war. He didn't need the political cover that the UN would have given him in March, and he still doesn't need it to justify the decision to go in. (Though if he doesn't get some UN cover now, to help him get out, he's going to have a very complicated re-election campaign.)

For all the problems after May 1, 2003, there is no thought that toppling Saddam was a mistake. And as for the absence of UN authorization, it's worth remembering that anytime the United States has felt that war was justified, it found a way of going into battle. Bush put together a coalition of sorts when efforts at the UN failed. In Vietnam, Lyndon Johnson had his Tonkin Gulf resolution after a fabricated incident. Nixon carried out an "incursion" in Cambodia with no one knowing except Henry Kissinger and the pilots who flew the bombing raids. We bombed Qaddhafi's personal homes after the Pan Am flight was brought down, we took out Noriega in Panama, we put down a rebellion in the Dominican Republic, we landed forces in Somalia, we fired missiles at what we thought was a bin Laden factory in Afghanistan. There are countless examples of America taking pre-emptive, unilateral action. And we are not alone. So have successive British governments in Northern Ireland, and so did Charles Hernu in New Zealand.

Let's be honest. Governments do what they are required to do for their countries' well being (though admittedly sometimes it's for a leader's self-interest). America went to war in Iraq with a clear disregard for the opinion of a number of its traditional allies. But one of those allies, the Germans, had overriding domestic reasons: Schröeder wanted to be re-elected. And it can be convincingly argued that France had domestic reasons too— because of the growing militancy of your Islamic population.

As far as domestic considerations and self-interest are concerned, take as an example not of the UN but the EU. France is ignoring the EU's stability and growth pact despite accords it has signed and in the face of strong disapproval of other members of the Union. That's not exactly like going to war, but there is a certain unmistakable disregard for partners in a fragile but vital cause.

One final point before we move on. When better dictionaries are written, maybe we'll have a better definition of Wilsonianism. The term has come to be shorthand for consultation and openness, for more of a multipolar approach to international governance than post–Cold War America has sometimes demonstrated. But, you know, Wilson wasn't exactly a model Wilsonian. He was no born-again Christian, he was a divine-right Christian. His interest in consultation was in converting people to his way of thinking, not at arriving at a consensus. And what he came to be known for mostly was naïveté.

COLOMBANI: At this point, we must mention the stakes again, beginning with the idea of the seriousness and viciousness of the current French-American discord, as well as the gravity of the transatlantic rift. It leads me to believe that once the Iraqi crisis is over, we will have to recreate a long-term joining of both sides of the Atlantic.

What are the challenges lying before us? There are two main questions on the floor. First, we must accept the fact that the United States did not invent the terrorism of Al-Qaida today, any more than it invented the Stalinism or Nazism of yesterday. The trauma of September 11 and the permanent threat that the US may be hit at any moment have been largely underestimated in Europe. So the first question is: Between Americans and Europeans, is there a long-term common vision of the world, or at least a similar one? Second question: Can we agree upon the nature of the threat and the best way to counter it?

Let's begin with the second question. Towards the end of 2003, *Le Monde* organized a debate during which French Foreign Minister Dominique de Villepin exclaimed, "There is no crisis!" between France and the United States. The proof he offered was the support France brought to the war against terrorism in the mobilization of French police and information networks. Villepin also enumerated the many points of agreement between the two nations. This was his demonstration that France and the US shared a common analysis without significant disagreement. I don't know if the Americans actually share this positive outlook.

The first question, meanwhile, lies in the very center of the divorce. On the one side, we have the good Jacques, herald of "multipolarity," and on the other, the bad George and his "unilateral" world. In fact, to say that the world must be multipolar is not the expression of policy, but rather the elaboration of a given. Multipolarity does not mean automatic security, or a more just world. By the same token, a unipolar world may depend on multilateral mechanisms, as Tony Blair advocates. The true, underlying difficulty, is to sound out hearts and minds. And is it not true, in fact, that the French position remains that the American superpower and its uses are a danger to peace and balance worldwide? In other words, doesn't France ultimately want to weaken the US? How else may one explain the desire to create an axis with Moscow?

This fear, like all other major considerations, goes back to the idea that we have of Europe. Should it continue to build an alliance with America, a partnership with her? Or should it become a counter-balance to the United States, even if it must build against America? It seems to me, that from Vedrine to Villepin, the idea of being a counter-balance wins. With Chirac, who knows? From this point of view, Alain Minc[72] is not wrong to suggest that if France follows this line of action, it would be following a dream as illusive as non-alignment was in the 1960s. In any event, France would be turning its back on an historical perspective that would allow it to share and participate in co-leadership, along with London and Berlin, in the construction of Europe.

After all, de Gaulle wanted to be a demanding and even sometimes uncompromising ally. And all British Prime Ministers want to be influential allies. Somewhere between the two, a European way must be forged. We should be looking for it together, rather than separately. That would imply that we agree on challenging the idea that Europe should construct itself against the United States. That would imply that France go back to respecting the rules of decency among allies. At the height of the quarrel over Mururoa and the resuming of French nuclear testing in Polynesia in 1995, Chirac was supported by London, Bonn and Washington in the name of a certain concept of alliance, whereas the rest of the world denounced France.

All in all, it has become urgent to elaborate a new partnership together. For me, first, we have to create a strategic doctrine that integrates the notion of development. Take for example the tragic fate of Africa, which concerns all of us. The rivalry that prevails with America is absurd, counter-productive and detrimental to Africans. Hence, development must be a key element in the policy.

Once again, this renewal would probably take place more smoothly if there is a leadership change. If he had the choice, a Frenchman would always choose the position of a Chirac, even when he exaggerates, over a Berlusconi or Aznar. Unfortunately, Bush's team will not change: It will continue to work with perfect cynicism towards the division of Europe.

The question is whether this rift will continue to widen, or whether new and sufficiently responsible leaders will believe that this line of thought is dangerous.

WELLS: I suppose there's another option—that the rift simply stays as it is. Stasis is possible in relations between two countries if it's carefully nurtured. And some level of stasis, though not the current level, which is pretty low, may even be necessary for a while once we get beyond our profound and virulent breach. I see photographs in the papers now of Bush and Chirac smiling together for the cameras. But a photo op is not a reconciliation. They're still playing a schoolyard game of who'll blink first, when perhaps they should instead make a serious effort to ignore each other.

Policy differences aside, it is frankly a mystery to me how the Bush administration has been so successful in demonizing France, and what is even more puzzling is how ripe America was for this vilification. I find it truly bewildering that in that diversity enriched, politically correct world it is acceptable and even chic to treat our oldest friend as our worst enemy. Ethnic jokes aren't allowed in America now—and shouldn't be. Except of course for jokes about the French.

I just read an interesting essay positing that the America of Bush feels more drawn to Germany than to France because both the US and Germany have "masculine" images—guns, BMWs, toughness. Whereas the identification of France is with the "feminine" pleasures—art, perfume, fashion, food. Perhaps, like men and women, the French and the Americans are figuratively from different planets.

The only possible insight I can bring to why America was so ripe for this derives from history. Colin Powell said we were partners who had been in marriage counseling for 225 years. At several times in our discussions, you have chided me for reliving old stories. Well, it is our mutual history that has paved the road that brought us to the present impasse. We don't have to relive de Gaulle and NATO, and we don't have to revisit Suez or Vietnam. But there is, through history, a surprisingly consistent refusal of the French to support America.

Now, we certainly do not want to revisit the pain and anguish of World War II and the Occupation, nor do we need to say another word about the place that D-Day has in the American psyche—not only is that enormous, but it has been reinforced for every generation with books (*The Longest Day*) and movies (*Saving Private Ryan*).

But there is something else about the period of Vichy, whose dark significance has, I think, grown in the American mind and affected the perception of France, even as actual memories of the war have faded. And that dark significance is the perceived extent to which the French helped in the extermination of the Jews. "Perceived," I said. I don't think you recognize how that looms among a very large segment of the American people. Not Joe Six-Pack, but leading opinion makers.

That is reinforced and complicated by France's historic ties to the Arab world, and it's complicated too by the impression that France does not move to stop the vandalism in Jewish cemeteries and the fires at synagogues. Yes, Chirac laid the wreath at the deportation memorial, and yes he accepted responsibility on behalf of the French people, and yes, he took criticism for that. France is not an anti-Semitic country—it most assuredly is not. I agree fully with the argument you made earlier that anti-Americanism has nothing whatsoever to do with anti-Semitism. But I hope you will take my point that for a large, articulate, influential body of American opinion, there is a direct correlation.

Time does not always heal wounds. In affairs of the heart and the human spirit, the passage of time doesn't always clarify things, it doesn't always allow impurities to settle to the bottom. And I think that in the past 50 years, some of the responsibility for the Holocaust has, in the American mindset, bled westward across the Rhine. Even if in the purest of truth there was no responsibility; even if in the purest of truth the extent of French collaboration was small; even if in the purest of truth everything about that perception is wrong: that's actually not enough.

France casts itself as a model. France holds up its values as superior and presents itself as a steadier beacon for aspiring democracies than America. France is the second or the first repository for universal truth—America being the other one. What surprise is there that when France calls America to account—over Iraq or whatever—Americans who remember the war and know French history riposte with reminders that at a time it mattered most, France failed to meet its own standards. The land that claims to have originated the concept of the rights of man should expect no less a riposte.

History is not something to be shut off. If we don't face up to history, I don't think we'll never get over it. Certainly my own country hasn't gotten over the truly awful consequences of slavery, no matter how much facing up we do. And the myth that de Gaulle helped create in the post-war years did not help France to face its responsibility and expiate its guilt. That it was bold and brave of Chirac to lay the wreath underscores my point.

COLOMBANI: The understanding that the French and Americans should share on globalization is that its first quality is the ability to widen the scope of democracy. Globalization is always viewed from an economic standpoint. As a synonym for international specialization, it is also a synonym for delocalization, and hence a move to rapidly accept what is now developing in Europe under the influence of the antiglobalizationists. Bearing in mind that globalization is also a synonym for the creation of wealth, albeit forced, as witnessed throughout Asia, Brazil, etc., the dialectic, along with antiglobalization criticism, should lead to a better organization of the international economy, and progress in planetary regulations.

The second understanding that should bring us all closer together is the certainty born with the history of the 20th century: Protectionism and nationalism produce war. And on the contrary, the development and liberalization of free trade are sources of progress and peace. The problem is that the US seems to have deviated from this belief, if not having completely turned its back on it.

The United States as well as Europe, must also redefine their concept of NATO, if only to better implement the transition that separates us from a veritable European defense program. In this respect, it seems to me that changing alliances becomes a dangerous game. On the one hand, we have the United States swearing in its alliance with Russia, as if Putin's Russia was the best ally. On the other hand, we have Chirac's efforts to constitute a Paris-Berlin-Moscow axis, which would only be as good as the great Democrat, Putin himself, would allow it to be. It's up to France to redefine exactly what it wants. Sometimes France seems to hesitate between adherence to the Arab league and its participation in the Atlantic alliance as a member who would want to be influential. This wide split is ridiculous and perfectly illusionary. The illusion may have been productive at one point, during the mobilization of public opinion against the war in Iraq. But it couldn't replace strategy. On the other hand, for the United States to use NATO as a weapon against the European Union is a devastating tactic.

I don't believe in a Paris-Berlin-Moscow alliance. I find the idea of giving one's blessing to the enterprise of recreating Soviet Russia mortifying. The reinstating of the Russian dictatorship is a mistake. All that, to counteract the Americans who seem to have decided to make Moscow their main supporter and to divide Europe. This is a no-win situation. Obviously, Europe has more to lose, but we will both lose. We have to re-think these strategic choices.

The fate of the Middle East will help or, on the contrary, make the international context even more unpredictable. If the US becomes part of the peace process once again in the Middle East, it would validate American strategy in the region and contradict the French counter-strategy based on Damascus, Arafat and on pan-Arabism, which is illusionary and increasingly anti-Semitic.

As France continues to criticize American policy, I fear that tomorrow we may be relegated to the position of many Arab states: condemned to pay lip-service and incapable of construction. Illusion may satisfy the national ego, but it is certainly not satisfactory for the future of France. And at the same time, I am confident. France is not wed to Chiracism. It has a high opinion of itself. It has incredible resources. It will play a positive role: Since de-colonization, more often than not, it has made the right choices at important moments.

WELLS: The American expression that is perhaps most apt is to "cut off your nose to spite your face." But there's an English expression that comes to mind, too, in this overall context: the "loyal opposition." Americans simply thought that Chirac's opposition on Iraq—right or wrong—was disloyal, and again I point to the example of Canada, a loyal ally that often disagrees, and particularly when America pursues an aggressive foreign policy.

It is the obsession with the United States that is distressing because, like you, Jean-Marie, I think it is self-destructive. It's damaging because it drains energy, and it's damaging also because it allows erroneous conclusions—like the conviction that the United States has laid out a grand scheme to destroy Europe and is using NATO, particularly, toward that end.

Peace and stability are in America's interests—peaceful and stable conditions within America's own borders, and across Europe as well. That's good for our economic well-being, for "life, liberty and the pursuit of happiness," words that fall too easily to our lips and too hard to our comprehension. Disuniting Europe is simply not in America's interests, not politically and not economically. We don't fear economic competition from Europe or anywhere else, because ours is an economy that thrives on competition and expands on free markets. In fact, restrictive tariffs—whether the ones that set off the Great Depression or Bush's recent, ill advised steel tariffs—cause the economy to stagnate and atrophy. Why ever would we fear competition from Europe? Most of the economic encouragement that America has given Europe over the last decade has been to enhance competitiveness, which inevitably means competition against the single dominant economy, America's own. Why? Because free markets are good—good for America and, not coincidentally, good for Europe too. NAFTA—pursued with vigor by the Clinton administration and supported rather dramatically by every living American president—exposed America to far more immediate competition than a united Europe will for a long, long time.

We are not trying to destroy Europe, but the obsession here with "America the Hegemon" transmogrifies into an obsession with "America the Evil." That has allowed Europeans to convince themselves that they are targets of this ogre.

Look: When Europe presents a united front on foreign policy, America will deal with Javier Solana or whoever is delegated to carry out the single policy. Until then, Henry Kissinger's pointed remark remains operative: Does Europe have a telephone number yet? Until it does, the United States will continue to deal with individual nations and not with an official in Brussels. That American policy is focused and European policy diffuse and still unformed is hardly the fault of America.

As to the quality of allies like Putin's Russia or Berlusconi's Italy, I hope we regard them as all God's children

America isn't trying to use NATO against Europe now any more than it did in the days of the cruise missiles or the Soviet gas pipeline across Eastern Europe and into France. Those disagreements were less divisive finally than this fight, but they were intense and sometimes bitter. Yet we remained allies.

We will this time. There is always that moment following a severe disagreement with your wife when the realization of how bloody-minded you have been sets in. On both sides in this split, there is already enough revisionism to let us see that process happening—the fall's literary scene in France has brought *La France qui tombe*,[73] and other books and journalistic examinations of France's failure to seize the European leadership, for example. And in America, as the 2004 presidential race takes shape, we have direct challenges to Bush about the intelligence that got us into war, the obduracy of the resistance, and how much it's costing.

Someday, when the Ba'aths are defeated and Iraq pacified, when the contracts for rebuilding the country are apportioned and when the Iraqis have a functioning, independent government under UN supervision, we will no doubt get back to the normal kind of fighting that we have always done.

Lexicon for the American Edition

Political Parties

Modern French politics remain characterized by a left-right division of the country even though the border between the two has been recently blurred. In the current Fifth Republic, begun by Charles de Gaulle, enormous executive power is given to the President, who is elected for seven years. His government is composed of a Council of Ministers, led by a Prime Minister. The legislative power, known as the Parliament, consists of the National Assembly (with 491 members, known as Deputés) and the Sénat (317 members, known as Sénateurs).

The Communist party, once a relatively powerful organization, almost disappeared concurrently with the fall of the Cold War. Simultaneously, the far right National Front's popularity has been fueled by high unemployment and rising nationalism, mostly against "les arabes," North Africans mainly from Algeria.

Besides the extremists (the Communist Party on the far left, and the National Front on the far right led by Jean-Marie Le Pen), several more moderate parties share the French political scene: the Union for the Presidential Majority (UMP, Jacques Chirac's party), which is relatively conservative; the French Democratic Union (UDF), which is closer to the center; the Socialist Party (PS, François Mitterrand's party); and the Greens Party, which is highly visible, but poorly represented in Congress.

The Unions

Although French unionism is less and less representative of workers, it still has a great deal of influence in the country. After World War II, the main workers' unions leaned more or less to the left. Among them are the General Workers Confederation (CGT), the French Workers Democratic Confederation (CFDT), the French Confederation of Christian Workers (CFTC), and Workers Force (FO).

A managements' union, the MEDEF, is characterized by political conservatism and economic liberalism.

Higher Education

After the Baccalaureat examination (a final exam at the end of secondary school, taken at around 18 years of age), the most prestigious opportunities are available through the "grandes ecoles." Universities, in fact, recruit without entrance exams or applications and studies are surprisingly inexpensive. The "grandes ecoles" are institutions that recruit by competitive exams, selecting the best candidates for their school. Among the most famous of these schools, are: the École nationale d'Administration (ENA), which trains high-ranking civil servants in government; the École des Hautes Études Commerciales (HEC), which is a business school; the École Polytechnique ("l'X"), a polytechnical school; the École Centrale, for scientific studies; and the École Normale Supérieure, for the liberal arts.

It is generally thought that attending one of these institutions opens the doors to the best careers.

Notes

1. Jacques Andreani, *L'Amerique et nous* (Odile Jacob 2000).
2. Justin Vaisse, "Etats-Unis: le regain francophobe," in *Politique internationale*, no. 97 (Fall 2002), p. 97.
3. Jonah Goldberg, columnist for the *National Review*, borrowed the expression from the television series *The Simpsons*.
4. January 22, 2003, American Secretary of Defense Donald Rumsfeld, declared that because France and Germany opposed conflict in Iraq, they represented the "old Europe" in his eyes.
5. United Nations Resolution 1441, which was approved unanimously on November 8, 2002. It outlined strict guidelines for weapons inspections in Iraq, with "serious consequences" for noncompliance.
6. Bill Keller, "The I-Can't-Believe-I'm-a-Hawk-Club," editorial in *The New York Times*, February 8, 2003.
7. Quai d'Orsay is the address of the French Ministry of Foreign Affairs.
8. *Vel d'hiv* is an abbreviation of Velodrome d'hiver, an indoor bicycle track in Paris where, during World War II, Jews were held before being sent to the camps.

9. The President of the Association of the Sons and Daughters of Jewish Deportees of France, Serge Klarsfeld, has dedicated his life to studying deportation and is a reference on the subject. In *Le Monde*, on the day commemorating the roundup at the Vel d'hiv, Klarsfeld stated that the attitude of the French during the Occupation explained how two-thirds of France's Jews survived (80,000 perished, whereas 240,000 survived), amounting to the "least terrible score of all major Jewish communities in Europe." He concluded his comments with 3 observations: "1. The anti-Semitic and xenophobic government of Vichy did not want to deport Jews and have them killed. It was more anti-Semitism by exclusion. 2. Confronted by complying to German demands, of which the ultimate goal was obvious, Vichy became an accomplice of the Third Reich in the summer of 1942, by arresting over 30,000 foreign Jews and their French children, and handing them over to the Gestapo for deportation. 3. Vichy would have continued massive cooperation through its police, had the French population in the Free Zone and France's religious leaders not put pressure on them to stop their criminal collaboration."

10. Before the onset of affirmative action, the Ivy League colleges in the Northeast United States had a tradition of discrimination and clandestine quotas for Jews and Blacks.

11. Quotation from the Scottish poet Robert Burns (1759-1796): "O, would some Power give us the gift to see ourselves as others see us."

12. "hard core"

13. Several political-financial scandals have occurred in France in the last 20 years, revealing collusion between senior politicians and certain industrial and financial groups. The Crédit Lyonnais is the largest nationalized French bank and Elf is the country's most important oil company. Walter Wells alludes to the consequences of State financial implications in

these companies and fiscal repercussions to tax-payers, resulting from their bankruptcy.

14. This 1919 song evokes the American soldiers returning from the First World War in Europe, finding home life insipid. It became a popular phrase, and even inspired the film *For Me and My Gal*, with Judy Garland and Gene Kelly.

15. Jean-François Revel (born 1925) is a journalist and columnist. He is the author of a pro-US defense, *L'Obsession anti-americaine*(Plon, 2002).

16. AMGOT (Allied Military Government of the Occupied Territories) sought to impose an allied military government in France upon its liberation in 1944, in order to ensure the transition for return to democracy.

17. José Bové is a French farmer, famous for his 1999 destruction of a McDonald's restaurant in his hometown of Millau. He is also the founder of the farmers union the Confederation Paysanne, and a long-time antiglobalization activist.

18. The Dardanelles Campaign took place from February 1915 to February 1916, being greatly encouraged by Churchill, then Lord of the Admiralty. The purposes of the attacks on the Turks in the Dardanelles were triple: to weaken the Ottoman Empire and protect Egypt (and the Suez Canal); to relieve the Russian Army from Turkish pressure in the Caucasus; and to open up the eastern front to divert the Germans. An offensive led by eighteen cavalrymen on March 18, 1915, resulted in a resounding defeat and the losses that ensued brought about the withdrawal of troops in the beginning of 1916.

19. Defined in 1823 by the fifth president of the United States, James Monroe, it specifies that the US must not intervene in the affairs of Europe and especially that Europe must not interfere in affairs on the American continent.

20. Expression used by American politicians in the 1840s to explain the continental expansion of the US. This notion included the idea of a mission: to bring the principle of liberty and democracy to other nations, but also the will to achieve economic self-sufficiency, which would bring freedom to Americans.
21. "Europe-USA: l'atout majeur," *Le Monde*, June 15–16, 2003.
22. Philip H. Gordon, "Bridging the Atlantic Divide," *Foreign Affairs*, January–February 2003.
23. Nelson Lund, "Capital Punishment in America," *The Public Interest*, Fall 2002.
24. The *"sang contamine"* scandal occurred in 1999 when three former government ministers—former Prime Minister Laurent Fabius, his former Social Affairs Minister Georgina Dufoix, and his former Health Minister Edmond Herve—were all charged with manslaughter for having allegedly known that the blood used in transfusions to over 3,600 hundred people in the mid-1980s was tainted. Many subsequently developed AIDS and died. Fabius and Dufoix were found innocent, and Herve was found guilty but was given no sentence.
25. Paul Touvier was a Vichy official in charge of a pro-Nazi militia. He was convicted in 1994 of having ordered the execution of seven Jews in 1944. Maurice Papon was a Vichy official who went on to serve as Prefect of Police under Charles de Gaulle and as budget minister under Valéry Gisgard d'Estaing. He was convicted in 1997 of having sent over 1,500 people to detention camps during the war. Most of those people subsequently died in Auschwitz.
26. In his *Of Paradise and Power: America and Europe in the New World Order* (Knopf, 2003).
27. Thomas Hobbes (1588–1679). English philosopher and author of *Leviathan*, was founder of a political school of thought where man in the state of nature was at war with

everyone and the world turned into chaos. Only a social contract founding a State could bring peace and order, on the condition that it be sufficiently authoritative.

28. North American Free Trade Agreement signed in 1994 by Canada, the US, and Mexico.

29. In 1768, France purchased Corsica from the Republic of Genoa. For the past few years, the island has gone through continuous nationalistic uprisings characterized by terrorist attacks (on institutions and private individuals, ordered by the underground independent party), with the purpose of obliging the State to grant independence. However supporters of independence in Corsica represent only a minority of the population.

30. The period of French history prior to the French Revolution, when the country was a monarchy.

31. 1802–1815 are the dates of the First Empire (Napoléon I); 1848–1870 are the dates of the Second Empire (Napoléon III).

32. Samuel P. Huntington proposed in his book *The Clash of Civilizations and the Remaking of World Order* (Simon & Schuster, 1996) that the world was comprised of several varied cultures in conflict and that Islam, in particular, was a problematic and hostile culture that saw itself in unavoidable conflict with Western culture.

33. Xavier de C***, Regis Debray. *L'Edit de Caracalla, ou plaidoyer pour des Etats-Unis d'Occident* (Fayard, 2002). Régis Debray (born 1940), author and philosopher, became a member of the Communist Party when he was very young and was adviser to President François Mitterrand from 1981 to 1984.

34. Francis Fukuyama, "Craquements dans le monde occidental," *Le Monde*, August 16, 2002.

35. Conservative Republican Senator from North Carolina.

36. Perspectives on World History and Current Events: www.geocities.com/pwhce/index.html.

37. Organization for Security and Cooperation in Europe, created in 1994 to accompany the end of the Cold War in Europe. It includes the US and 55 European states.
38. The Asia-Pacific Economic Cooperation, founded in 1989 for the purpose of facilitating economic exchanges with countries in the Far East
39. See Joseph Nye, *The Paradox of American Power: Why the World's Only Superpower Can't Go It Alone* (Oxford University Press, 2002).
40. "The Benevolent Europe," *Foreign Policy*, Summer 1998.
41. George W. Bush, "Speech at the University of Warsaw," June 15, 2001.
42. Denis Lacorne (editor) et alia. *L'Amerique dans les tetes, un siecle de fascinations et d'aversions* (Hachette, 1984), p.19.
43. The government installed by Napolean Bonaparte for the three years from his ascendancy until his declaration of the First Empire; it was led by three consuls.
44. In support of politics that are cooperative with the United States.
45. The first French trade union, established in 1895.
46. As secretary general, Blondel is leader of the Force Ovrière.
47. The *Bottin mondain*, a French social registry that lists the names and addresses of the social elite.
48. French jazz and pop composer, best known for his scores for movies of the 1960s and 70s such as *The Thomas Crown Affair* and *The Umbrellas of Cherbourg*.
49. The S.O.E. (Special Operations Executive) was a British secret service formed shortly after France's defeat to encourage resistance among the civilian populations in occupied Europe, and to promote sabotage and subversion. S.O.E. operations in France were directed by two territorial sections based in London: Section F, under British control and Section RF, which was in liaison with the FFL (the *Forces Francais libres,* or Free French Forces) under General de Gaulle.
50. A graduate of the École nationale d'Administration.

51. Founder of the McDonald's restaurant chain.
52. William S. Paley (1901–1990), was the long-time head of the major American television network CBS.
53. Louis de Funes (1914–1983), French comic actor.
54. From Washington's Farewell Address, a speech that was never given but released by Washington to the press and first published September 19, 1796.
55. Horatio Alger (1832–1899), American novelist who wrote for adolescents, creating heroes who always achieve great success due to their determination and luck.
56. Character in Arthur Miller's play *Death of a Salesman* (1949).
57. "the American drift"
58. The New Deal was the name given to the domestic programs of President Franklin Roosevelt, and the Fair Deal was the name given to the domestic programs of his successor, President Harry S. Truman.
59. Harcourt, Brace & Company, 1922.
60. Pleasantville is a common expression designating a charming, pleasant suburb where nothing ever happens and is rather boring. Used as a film title (1998), it constantly refers to a vision of happy American suburbia represented in the sitcoms of the 1950s.
61. Character from Martin Scorsese's film *Taxi Driver* (1976), played by Robert de Niro. Travis Bickle is a violent taxi driver who is rejected by society and ultimately commits several murders.
62. "Don't touch my wallet, or my time off."
63. "Every man for himself."
64. *Le Figaro*, May 30, 2003.
65. Bush's first State of the Union Address, given January 29, 2002.
66. John Maynard Keynes (1883–1946), influential British economist and author of *The General Theory of Employment, Interest and Money* (1936), one of the seminal books on economics in the 20th Century.

67. George Kennan (1904–) American diplomat and historian. A key player in post-war politics, he is best known for his theory of containment with regards to the USSR; for playing a major role in Japan's reconstruction; and for his role in the implementation of the Marshall Plan in Europe.

68. Article in the July, 1947 issue of *Foreign Affairs*, written anonymously by George Kennan, in which he advocated the policy of containment, which would ultimately become the US blueprint for the Cold War.

69. George Kennan, *Foreign Affairs*, XXV, No.4, July 1947, 566–82.

70. "Give and take."

71. Phrase used by President George H.W. Bush to describe the geopolitical situation after the first Gulf War.

72. In his *Le Nouveau Moyen Âge* (Gallimard, 1993).

73. Nicolas Baverez, *La France qui tombe* (Perrin, 2003).

Selected Bibliography

Nos Amis les Français, Guide pratique à l'usage des GI's en France 1944-45, Paris: Le Cherche Midi, 2003.

SERFATY, Simon, *La France vue par les Etats-Unis: Réflexions sur la Francophobie à Washington*, Institut Français des Relations Internationales, Paris, 2002.

KORB, Lawrence J., *A New National Security Strategy: In an Age of Terrorists, Tyrants and Weapons of Mass Destruction*, New York: Council on Foreign Relations, 2003.

KAGAN, Robert, *Of Paradise and Power, America and Europe in the New World Order*, New York: Alfred A. Knopf, 2003.

POLLACK, Kenneth M., *The Threatening Storm: The Case for Invading Iraq*, New York: Random House, 2002.

HAASS, Richard N., "Multilateralism for a Global Era," Remarks to the Carnegie Endowment for International Peace / Center on International Cooperation Conference, November 14, 2001.

POWELL, Secretary Colin L., "Remarks at the World Economic Forum," Davos, Switzerland, January 26, 2003.

KAGAN, Robert, "The Benevolent Empire," *Foreign Policy*, New York : Summer 1998.

COGAN, Charles G., *Oldest Allies, Guarded Friends: The United States and France since 1940*, Westport: Praeger, 1994.

HOGE Jr., James F. and Gideon ROSE, eds. *How Did This Happen? Terrorism and the New War*, New York: Public Affairs, 2001.

STANGER, Ted, *Sacrés Français: Un Américain nous regarde*, Paris: Editions Michalon, 2003.

MAILER, Norman, *Why Are We At War?*, New York: Random House Trade Paperbacks, 2003.

ZAKARIA, Fareed, *The Future of Freedom: Illiberal Democracy at Home and Abroad*, New York: W.W. Norton & Company, April 2003.

Index

JEAN-MARIE COLOMBANI
is the editor in chief of France's leading newspaper, *Le Monde,* and heads the board of directors for *La Vie-Le Monde,* a syndicate of over thirty newspapers. He is the author of numerous books, including *Portrait du président ou le monarque imaginaire* (1985), *Le Mariage blanc,* with Jean-Yves Lhomeau, (1986), *La France sans Mitterrand* (1992), *La Gauche survivra-t-elle aux socialistes?* (1994), *De la France en général et de ses dirigeants en particulier* (1996), *Le Résident de la République* (1998), *Les Infortunes de la République* (2000), and *Tous Américains?* (2002).

WALTER WELLS
has been managing editor and deputy editor of the Paris-based daily *The International Herald Tribune* since 1980. He left the newspaper in 2001 but was recalled to serve as executive editor two years later by *The New York Times* when it acquired full ownership. Before 1980 he worked as an editor on the national desk of *The New York Times.* He and his wife, the cookbook author Patricia Wells, have lived in France since 1980. He has been a lecturer at *l'Institute d'Etudes Politiques* and at le *Centre de Perfectionnement des Journalistes,* and is a member of the Council on Foreign Relations.

LUC JACOB-DUVERNET
is a veteran newspaper and magazine editor who founded the publishing and communications company SFG (Société des Fondateurs de Génération), as well as the Éditions Jacob-Duvernet publishing house, which specializes in books on current events and politics. He is the author of several books, including *Le Miroir des Princes* (1994) and *La République des Artisans* (1999).